LATER PREHISTORIC AND ROMANO-BRITISH BURIAL AND SETTLEMENT AT HUCCLECOTE, GLOUCESTERSHIRE EXCAVATIONS IN ADVANCE OF THE GLOUCESTER BUSINESS PARK LINK ROAD, 1998

by Alan Thomas, Neil Holbrook and Clifford Bateman

with contributions by
Helen S. Bowstead Stallybrass, Nina Crummy, Peter Guest, Emma Harrison, Fiona Roe, Tracy Stickler, Jane Timby, Alan Vince, Tony Waldron, Graeme Walker and Tim Young

COTSWOLD ARCHAEOLOGY
Bristol and Gloucestershire Archaeological Report No. 2

By agreement with Cotswold Archaeology this report is distributed free
to members of the Bristol and Gloucestershire Archaeological Society
To accompany Volume 121 of the Society's *Transactions* for 2003

BRISTOL AND GLOUCESTERSHIRE ARCHAEOLOGICAL REPORT NO. 2

© Authors and Cotswold Archaeological Trust Ltd, 2003
Building 11, Kemble Enterprise Park, Cirencester, Glos. GL7 6BQ

All rights reserved. No part of this publication may be reproduced, stored in a retrieval system, or transmitted in any form or by any means electronic, photocopying, recording or otherwise without the prior permission of Cotswold Archaeological Trust Ltd.

ISSN 1479-2389
ISBN 09523196 7 5
Cotswold Archaeological Trust Ltd.
Building 11
Kemble Enterprise Park
Cirencester, Glos. GL7 6BQ

Series Editor: Martin Watts
Produced by Cotswold Archaeological Trust Ltd, Cirencester
Printed by Trio Graphics Ltd, Gloucester

CONTENTS

Contents 1

Abstract 2

Acknowledgements 2

Introduction 3

Excavation Results 8

The Radiocarbon Dates 30

The Finds 31

The Biological Evidence 56

Discussion 62

Bibliography 68

ABSTRACT

Excavations in advance of the construction of the Gloucester Business Park Link Road, Hucclecote, in 1998 revealed alluvium deposited by the Horsbere Brook, in places up to 2m deep. Radiocarbon dating demonstrates that the alluvium had been deposited by the 12th century BC. Three or four Middle Bronze Age cremation burials were probably part of a flat cemetery, the site subsequently occupied by a Late Bronze Age or Early Iron Age settlement which contained in excess of four post-built roundhouses. In the 1st century AD a settlement that contained a number of probable mass-walled roundhouses was constructed. It was extensively reorganised in the early 2nd century when a series of ditched enclosures were linked to Ermin Street by a 320m-long trackway. A small cemetery of 12 inhumations is noteworthy as it demonstrates that the Late Iron Age tradition of burial by crouched inhumation persisted into the 2nd century AD. Several of the burials were accompanied by grave goods, and one of the males suffered from a very rare form of dwarfism to his forearms, a condition that would have been obvious to his contemporaries. The settlement continued in use until the late 3rd or early 4th century, although the trackway ditches continued to accumulate material into the later 4th century. The trackway and enclosures appear to have survived as visible earthworks into the medieval period as their orientation influenced the alignment of medieval field systems.

ACKNOWLEDGEMENTS

The evaluation and excavation were commissioned by Arlington Securities plc via their agents MacGregor Smith and main contractor Kier Group. The geophysical survey of the road corridor was undertaken by Stratascan. The geophysical survey of the neighbouring area by GSB, and subsequent evaluation by Cotswold Archaeology in 2000, were commissioned by CPM on behalf of Bryant Homes. We are grateful to GSB for allowing us to reproduce their findings in this report. Thanks are due to Michael Smith (MacGregor Smith), Alasdair Higgs (Kier Group), Matthew Watkins (Arlington Securities) and Royston Clark (CPM) for their assistance and support. The interest and useful suggestions of Charles Parry of Gloucestershire County Council Archaeology Section, who monitored the project on behalf of Tewkesbury Borough Council, were also appreciated.

The evaluation and excavation in advance of the road were directed in the field by Clifford Bateman, assisted by Mark Brett, and were managed by Mark Leah. The stratigraphic account was written by Alan Thomas, assisted by Clifford Bateman, and managed in turn by Mark Leah and Neil Holbrook. The evaluation in 2000 was directed by Alan Thomas and managed by Neil Holbrook. We are grateful to all the staff who worked on the project, and to all the individuals who have contributed to this report. Jane Timby thanks Dr Alan Vince for undertaking the petrological analysis of the prehistoric sherd. The thin-section analysis was prepared by Paul Hands, Department of Earth Sciences, University of Birmingham, and the ICPS analysis was carried out by Dr N. Walsh, Department of Geology, Royal Holloway College, Egham. The illustrations were produced by Peter Moore. Earlier drafts were read by Tim Darvill and Richard Reece and the authors are grateful for their comments. The finds and archive will be deposited with Gloucester City Museum under accession number GLRCM 1998/32.

INTRODUCTION

In 1996, planning permission was granted by Tewkesbury Borough Council for a link road between the Brockworth bypass and the former Gloucester Trading Estate which was in the process of being developed as a business park. A condition attached to the permission stated that a programme of archaeological fieldwork was required prior to the commencement of construction as the road lay in an area of archaeological potential, approximately 5.5km east of Gloucester and a little to the north of Ermin Street, the major Roman road to Cirencester and beyond (Fig. 1). A Roman settlement has been excavated at Brockworth, 700m east of the site (Rawes 1981), and Hucclecote Roman villa lies 650m to the west, close to the Horsbere Brook (Clifford 1933 and 1961). Archaeological fieldwork undertaken within the immediate vicinity of the villa revealed further Romano-British buildings, a corn dryer and a complex system of enclosures (Parry 1994; Parry and Cook 1995; Sermon 1997). It was conceivable that these agricultural features might extend into the road corridor. The potential was further highlighted in 1998 by a gradiometer survey on either side of the road in connection with a different development, which revealed a previously unknown settlement complex of putative Iron Age or Romano-British date (GSB 1998; Fig. 2).

A brief for archaeological evaluation of the link road corridor was prepared by the Senior Archaeological Officer of Gloucestershire County Council and Cotswold Archaeological Trust (CAT; now Cotswold Archaeology (CA)) was commissioned by Arlington Securities plc to undertake the project. The first stage of the project consisted of a magnetometer survey over the proposed road corridor. This established the presence of enclosure and boundary ditches and other discrete anomalies. A programme of trial trenching, consisting of sixteen 30m-long trenches (a 2% sample of the application area), followed to investigate these features. This established the presence of a Romano-British settlement linked to Ermin Street by a ditched trackway (Bateman 1998).

In response to the evaluation results a project design to excavate the route of the road was issued by CAT and approved by Tewkesbury Borough Council acting upon the advice of Gloucestershire County Council. As part of this design it was agreed that topsoil stripping should be undertaken only within the area designated for the road cutting with the roadside embankments being formed directly upon intact topsoil horizons, allowing the *in situ* preservation of archaeological deposits beneath.

The topsoil and subsoil along the route of the road cutting were mechanically stripped under archaeological supervision. In addition, where the evaluation had identified significant archaeological survival, the fill of medieval furrows was also removed by machine to ensure full exposure of underlying deposits. Discrete features such as pits and postholes were at a minimum half-sectioned and 20% of linear features were sampled. All identified burials and structural features were fully excavated. A full written, drawn and photographic record was maintained. Following completion of the site works an assessment was made of the main findings and a programme of analysis and research proposed (Bateman 1999). This strategy was approved by Gloucestershire County Council, and this report presents the results of the excavation and post-excavation phases.

Subsequently, between August and September 2000, CAT carried out a further archaeological evaluation consisting of 39 trenches to the west and east of the Link Road as part of a separate planning application (Fig. 2). This work confirmed the results of the gradiometer survey undertaken in 1998.

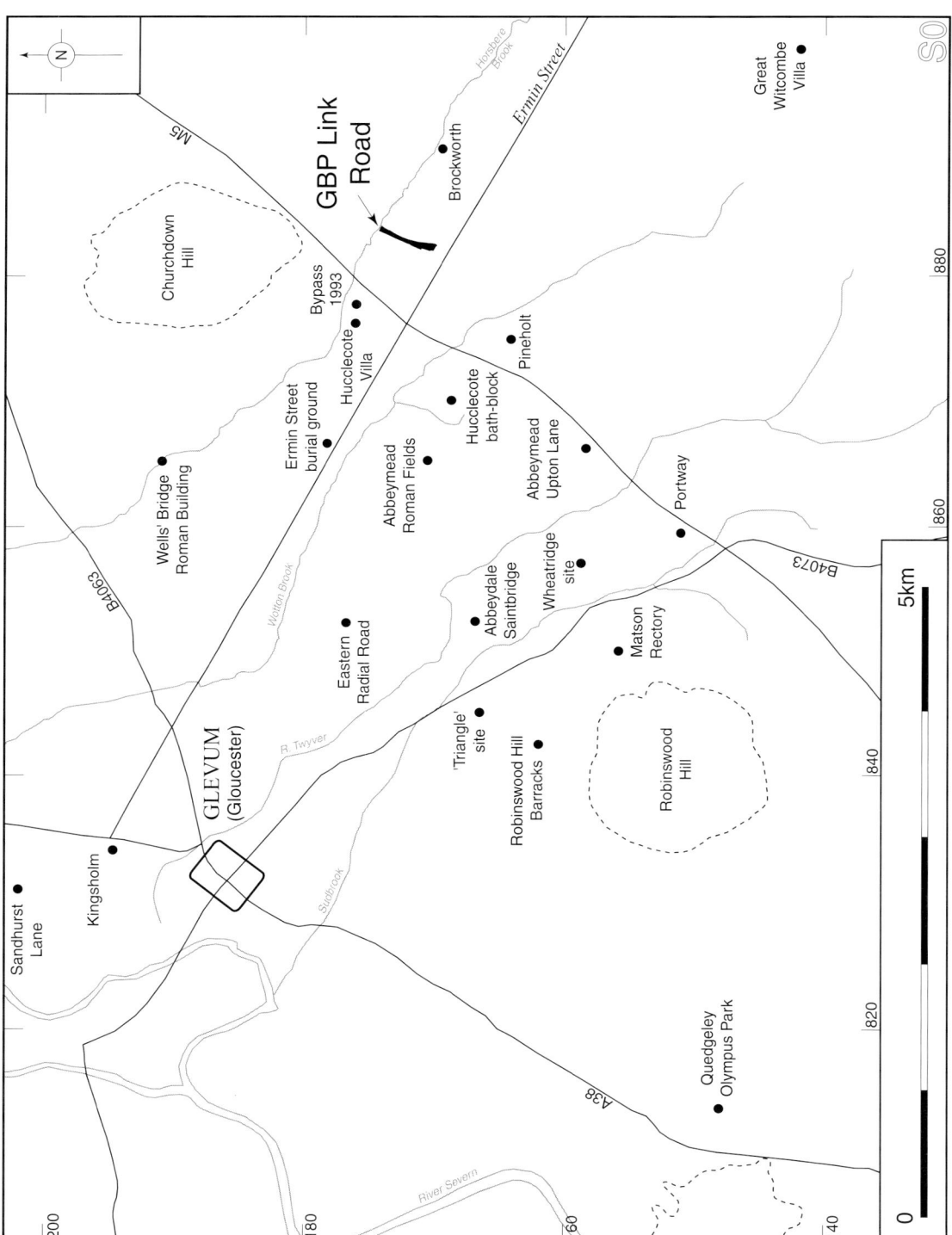

Fig. 1: Location plan (scale 1:50,000)

Location, topography and geology

The excavation extended north from the junction of Hucclecote Road and the Barnwood Bypass as far as the Horsbere Brook (NGR: SO 8824 1700 to SO 8838 1742) and comprised an area of 3.6ha (Fig. 2). The site consisted of agricultural land, previously under arable cultivation, bounded to the east and west by further fields. It sloped gently from approximately 45.3m AOD in the south to 41.7m AOD in the north towards the Horsbere Brook. This brook is one of a number of small streams and rivers which flow broadly north-westwards from the Cotswold escarpment 3km to the east of the site to join the River Severn in the general vicinity of Gloucester (Fig. 1).

The natural geology comprised clays belonging to the broad mass of the Lower Lias beds capped in places by eroded remnants of the Third or Main terrace gravels. Across most of the site these natural deposits were sealed by alluvium which increased in thickness towards, and was presumably derived from, the Horsbere Brook.

Preservation and phasing

The site had been severely truncated by the furrows of three separate medieval ridge and furrow ploughing regimes (Fig. 3). These had the initial effect of masking archaeological deposits. Over much of the site the furrows were removed during machining although this process inevitably led to the further truncation of some deposits. The furrows had clearly removed many archaeological features, such as some of the postholes of the prehistoric structures described below, although their effect on deeper features was less marked. Conversely the headlands and plough ridges created during the ploughing had the effect of preserving archaeological deposits beneath. It is of note that the Romano-British cemetery (Period 4.3) lay adjacent to a post-medieval hedge boundary on the same alignment. It is possible that these burials, which lay at a shallow depth, were preserved because they were less prone to the effects of modern ploughing.

The general impression gained from the fills of the prehistoric and Romano-British features described below is that most had silted naturally over time, although there were features such as midden 2848 (Period 4.3) which had obviously been deliberately backfilled. However, towards the northern end of the excavation it is clear that there had been episodic flooding from the Horsbere Brook as the fills contained varying degrees of alluvial silts. This was most marked in the fills of ditch 3283 (Period 4.3) and depression 3386, where the fills consisted completely of alluvial silts. Elsewhere, Enclosure C (Period 4.3) contained a lesser degree of alluvial silts within the fill of its boundary ditch.

The phasing of the archaeological deposits described below was carried out on the basis of stratigraphy, ceramic dating and, to a small extent, radiocarbon dating. However, there were inevitable problems in the ceramic sequence caused by the conservative nature of the pottery assemblage, particularly with the Severn Valley wares which made up much of the assemblage. This has led to the creation of just three Romano-British phases with the third being particularly long-lived, lasting from the 2nd to the 4th centuries AD.

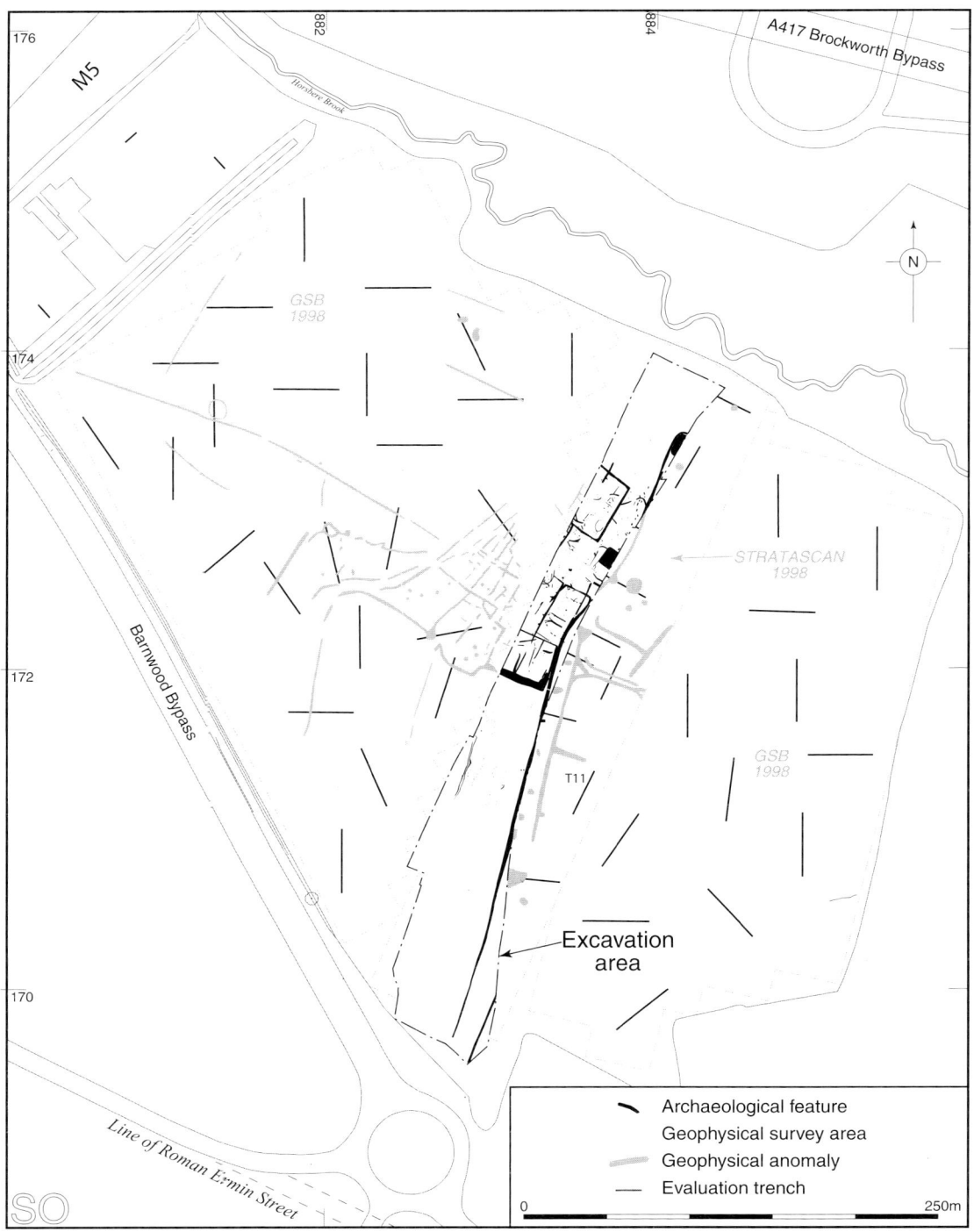

Fig. 2: Excavation area, evaluation trenches and anomalies from the geophysical surveys (scale 1:4000)

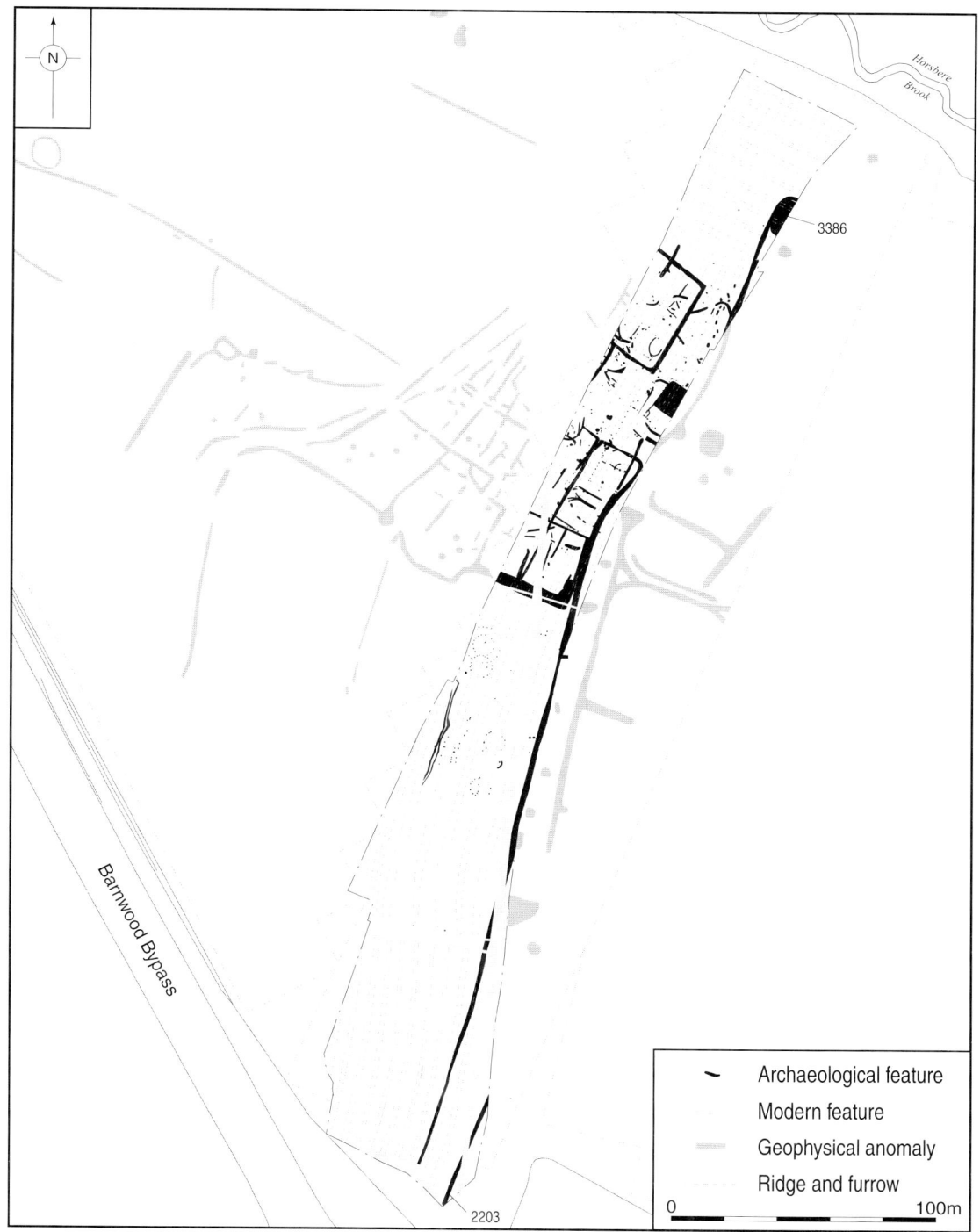

Fig. 3: All feature plan (scale 1:2500)

EXCAVATION RESULTS

Summary of the principal archaeological periods

Period 1:   post-glacial alluviation
Period 2:   Middle Bronze Age cremations (*c.*14th to 12th century BC)
Period 3:   Late Bronze Age/Early to Middle Iron Age settlement (*c.* 1100 to 400 BC)
Period 4.1:   Romano-British settlement (1st century AD)
Period 4.2:   Romano-British settlement (early 2nd century AD)
Period 4.3:   Romano-British burials; ditched enclosures; trackway (2nd to early 4th century AD)
Period 5:   medieval agriculture

In the following account n.i. indicates that a feature is not illustrated.

Period 1: post-glacial alluviation

In evaluation trench 11 (Fig. 2) the natural gravels were covered by a 0.1m-thick red-brown gravelly clay, possibly an original ground surface. This was cut by six small subcircular features which were interpreted as being of natural (possibly tree-throw holes) rather than cultural origin. These were in turn covered by 1.25m of alluvium within which three distinct horizons could be observed. Just to the north-east of the excavation area immediately adjacent to the Horsbere Brook a machine-cut section, excavated by contractors, revealed the alluvium to be over 2m deep with evidence of a major channel and braided water courses filled with clays, silts and sands. The alluvium gradually becomes shallower to the south away from the brook and for the southernmost 100m of the excavation area none was apparent. However, nearly all of the archaeological features described below are cut into the uppermost level of the alluvium. One produced a residual microlith, possibly of Mesolithic date.

Period 2: Middle Bronze Age cremations (*c.* 14th to 12th century BC) (Figs 4 and 5)

A single residual sherd of Early Bronze Age Beaker was found in fill 2269 of Romano-British grave B3 (Fig. 8), but the earliest features date to the Middle Bronze Age when part of the site was used as a cremation cemetery. No associated settlement features were found although there was a widespread distribution of residual pottery dating to this period.

A group of three cremations (Burials 1, 5 and 8) was found *c.* 275m south of the Horsbere Brook and, approximately 95m to the north-east of these, part of a cremation urn (Burial 17, n.i.) was recovered from an isolated pit. Burial 1 was of an adult and was found in a pit which measured 0.75m in diameter and 0.16m deep. The cremation was in primary fill 2240 which consisted largely of charcoal, presumably debris from the funeral pyre. Two radiocarbon dates from the charcoal produced results of 1413–1128 cal. BC and 1388–1000 cal. BC which suggest burial occurred in the 14th to 12th century BC. A secondary fill of a grey-brown sandy clay covered the cremation. Burial 5 was in a pit of similar dimensions to Burial 1. The bone was of an adult and was contained in a Middle Bronze Age cremation urn of which mostly only basesherds survived. Burial 8 was found in a pit which measured 0.4m in diameter and 0.22m deep and

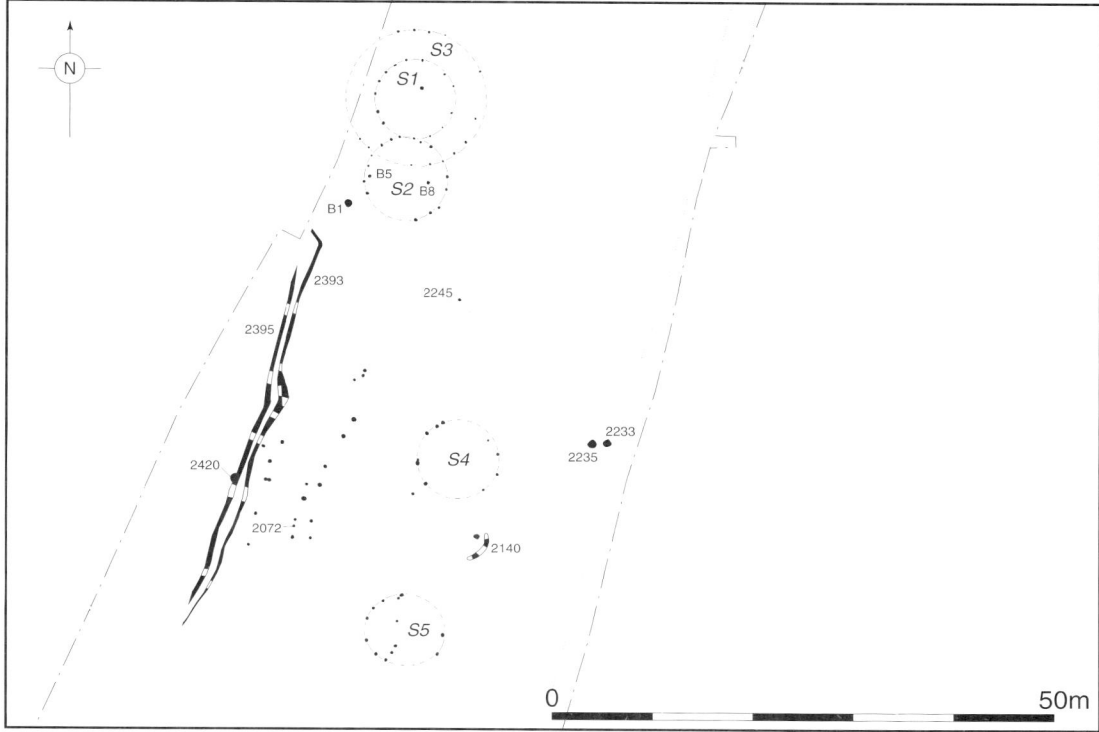

Fig. 4: Periods 2 and 3 features (scale 1:750)

contained a single fill of cremated adult bone mixed with an orange-brown silty clay with charcoal. Burial 17 consisted of the base sherds of a Middle Bronze Age biconical cremation urn and was found in a pit which measured 1.52m in diameter and 0.2m deep (n.i.). No skeletal material was found. Approximately 28m to the north-east posthole 3056 (n.i.) also produced a potential Middle Bronze Age potsherd.

Nineteen sherds of residual Middle Bronze Age pottery were also found across the site. In addition, 39 thick-walled potsherds with a calcareous paste (fabric CALC1), possibly of Middle or Late Bronze Age date, were also recovered. Despite the small quantity, the pottery and cremations suggest further Middle Bronze Age activity in the area.

Period 3: Late Bronze Age/Early to Middle Iron Age settlement (*c.* 11th to 5th century BC) (Figs 4 and 5)

Overlying the Period 2 cremations was one of four or possibly five post-built roundhouses. The position of the doorways could not be reliably ascertained for any of the houses. A linear gully and possible fence boundaries also belong in this period, as may a curvilinear gully in the northern part of the site.

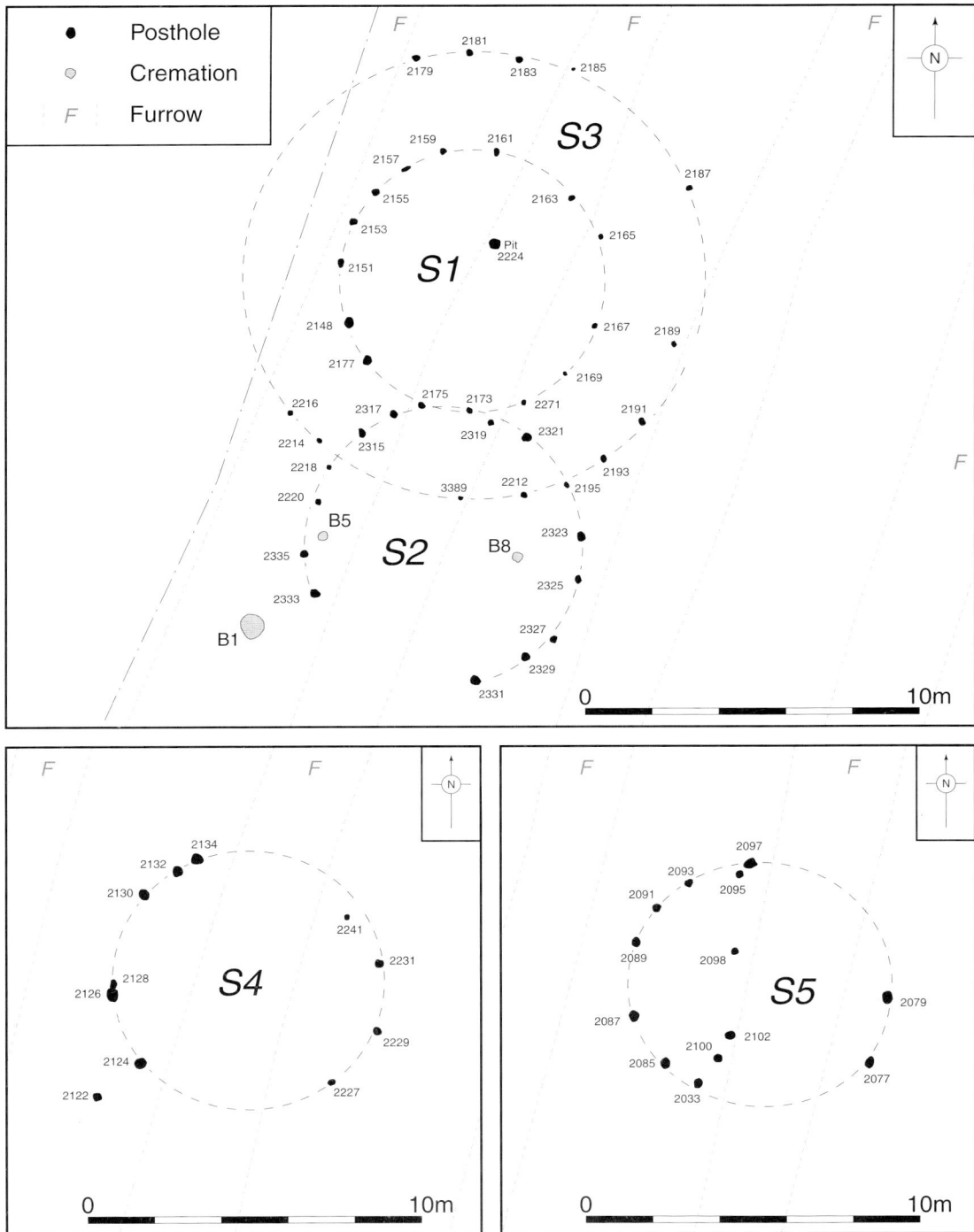

Fig. 5: Period 3 roundhouses (scale 1:200)

The roundhouses

Structure 3 (S3) measured 14m in diameter and consisted of a ring of 12 or 13 postholes between 0.03m and 0.12m deep. No dating evidence was recovered although a small quantity of non-ferrous slag was found in posthole 2189. Lying concentrically within Structure 3 was another post-ring termed Structure 1 (S1), which may represent an internal support for Structure 3 or an entirely separate structure which was either earlier or later than Structure 3. Structure 1 measured 8.1m in diameter and consisted of a ring of 13 to 15 postholes between 0.1m and 0.2m deep. Late Bronze Age or Early Iron Age potsherds were found in postholes 2151, 2157 and 2159, and posthole 2148 produced a sherd that probably derives from the cremation urn of Burial 5. A piece of oak from fill 2166 of posthole 2165 produced a radiocarbon date of 787–399 cal. BC. A small quantity of non-ferrous slag was also found in posthole 2165 and part of a saddle quern, possibly used as packing material, was found in posthole 2167. The fill 2223 of a small pit 2224 within the interior of either Structure 1 or Structure 3 contained charred material from which two radiocarbon dates of 760–385 cal. BC and 761–262 cal. BC were obtained.

Structure 2 (S2) measured 8.2m in diameter and consisted of a ring of 13 to 16 postholes between 0.15 and 0.25m deep. Its stratigraphic relationship with Structures 1 and 3 was not resolved.

Structure 4 (S4) measured 8m in diameter and consisted of ten postholes between 0.08m and 0.22m deep, of which 2126, 2134 and 2227 contained Late Bronze Age or Early Iron Age potsherds. It was cut by a medieval plough furrow. Structure 5 (S5) measured 7.9m in diameter and consisted of a ring of nine to ten postholes between 0.11m and 0.24m deep, of which 2087 produced Late Bronze Age or Early Iron Age pottery. It was cut by the same furrow as Structure 4. Three internal postholes (2102, 2098 and 2100) were also identified and posthole 2100 contained pottery of this period.

Other features

To the south and west of Structures 1 to 5 were two 45m-long parallel, north-east/south-west-aligned sinuous gullies 2393 and 2395 which were 0.16m and 0.1m deep respectively. The former turned to the north-west at its northern end. The relationship between these gullies, which were between 0.2m and 1.1m apart, is uncertain, although both contained Late Bronze Age or Early Iron Age potsherds, as did 0.46m-deep pit 2420, which cut gully 2395.

A group of postholes, typically 0.06m to 0.4m deep, was found immediately to the east of and broadly parallel to the gullies. More may have been removed by a furrow which cut through this group but it is possible that they formed part of successive fence boundaries. One posthole (2072) produced pottery of this period as did posthole 2245 to the north-east. Further undated postholes were also found to the east of Structures 1 to 5, along with two very shallow pits 2233 and 2235 with scorched sides, the fills of which contained mostly charcoal. Between Structures 4 and 5 was 0.42m-deep curvilinear gully 2140 which contained a potsherd of this period, amongst an otherwise Middle Bronze Age assemblage.

Approximately 150m to the north-east of Structures 1 to 5 was short 0.2m-deep curvilinear gully 3199 (n.i.), which contained two potsherds of this period. Its function is unclear although it may form the remnants of a roundhouse drip gully. Nearby posthole 3255 (n.i.) produced three sherds of the same date. A small quantity of residual pottery of this period was also found widely spread in the northern part of the site.

A crouched burial (Burial 2; Fig. 9) was found approximately 160m to the north-east of Structures 1 to 5. The burial is of a different character, and is isolated from, the Romano-British inhumations on the site. The latter burials also contained abundant sherds of Roman pottery within the grave fills, whereas no finds were recovered from the fill of this burial. As such it has tentatively been assigned to Periods 2 or 3, although its location is marked on Fig. 6 for convenience.

Grave: Burial 2 was found in a grave aligned north-east to south-west measuring 0.9m x 0.44m across and 0.1m deep. It lay on its left side with both hands slightly under the jaw. It produced no dating evidence.
Skeleton, by Tony Waldron: Adult of unknown sex, aged between 35 and 45 at the time of death. The skeleton was very fragmentary and it was not possible to take any measurements or to determine the likelihood of any pathology in the post-cranial skeleton. The teeth showed evidence of enamel hypoplasia which probably indicated some illness during childhood, perhaps an infectious disease such as measles or chickenpox. There were dental caries affecting the left lower first molar and the right lower first premolar.

Period 4: Romano-British settlement and cemetery (*c.* 1st to 4th century AD)

Romano-British activity on the site can be divided into three broad periods spanning the 1st to 4th centuries AD.

Period 4.1: 1st century AD (Fig. 6)
No clear evidence of immediate pre-conquest activity was found with the possible exception of pit 3273 (see below). However, a possible enclosure and several small pits, postholes and gullies produced ceramics that were current in the 1st and 2nd centuries AD.

Curvilinear gullies (possible roundhouses)
The stratigraphic relationship between 70mm-deep linear gully 2640 and 0.26m-deep curvilinear gully 2409, with a north-facing terminal, was not established. The function of the latter, which was cut by pit 2613, is unclear although its projected diameter of 11m to 12m suggests that it may have formed part of the drip gully of a possible roundhouse (?RH1), with a north-east-facing entrance. To the south, 0.28m-deep pit 2787 also produced pottery of this period as did 0.12m-deep posthole 2758 to the north-east. Several undated postholes were also found to the west of the gully. Some 20m to the north-east of ?RH1 was another shallow curvilinear gully 2899. The course of this gully was difficult to trace in excavation but it is possible that it curved to the north to meet 0.22m deep gully 3252. Once again it is possible that these may have formed a drip gully, with a diameter of approximately 11m, for a roundhouse (?RH2). Just to the north of gully 3252 were three shallow intercutting pits (3125, 3218 and 3220) with pottery of this period being recovered from pit 3125. Several undated postholes were found to the west of this gully. The short curvilinear gully 3248, 0.18m deep, might indicate a third roundhouse (?RH3). A sherd of Malvernian limestone-tempered pottery was found in its fill and an adjacent pit 3250 contained part of a pillar-moulded glass bowl of 1st century AD date along with sherds of Severn Valley ware pottery.

Enclosure A, gullies and pits
This possible enclosure was aligned north-west to south-east as opposed to the prevailing north-east to south-west alignment of the later phases of Romano-British ditches and enclosures. Its north-eastern corner was defined by 0.33m-deep ditch 3036 which had been recut once (Fig. 14, section 3). It terminated to the south-west but, after a gap of 2.7m, continued for a short length as 0.26m-deep ditch 2921. Little else survived of the enclosure ditch although the south-western side may be represented by 0.12m-deep ditch 2976, which would mean that the enclosure was

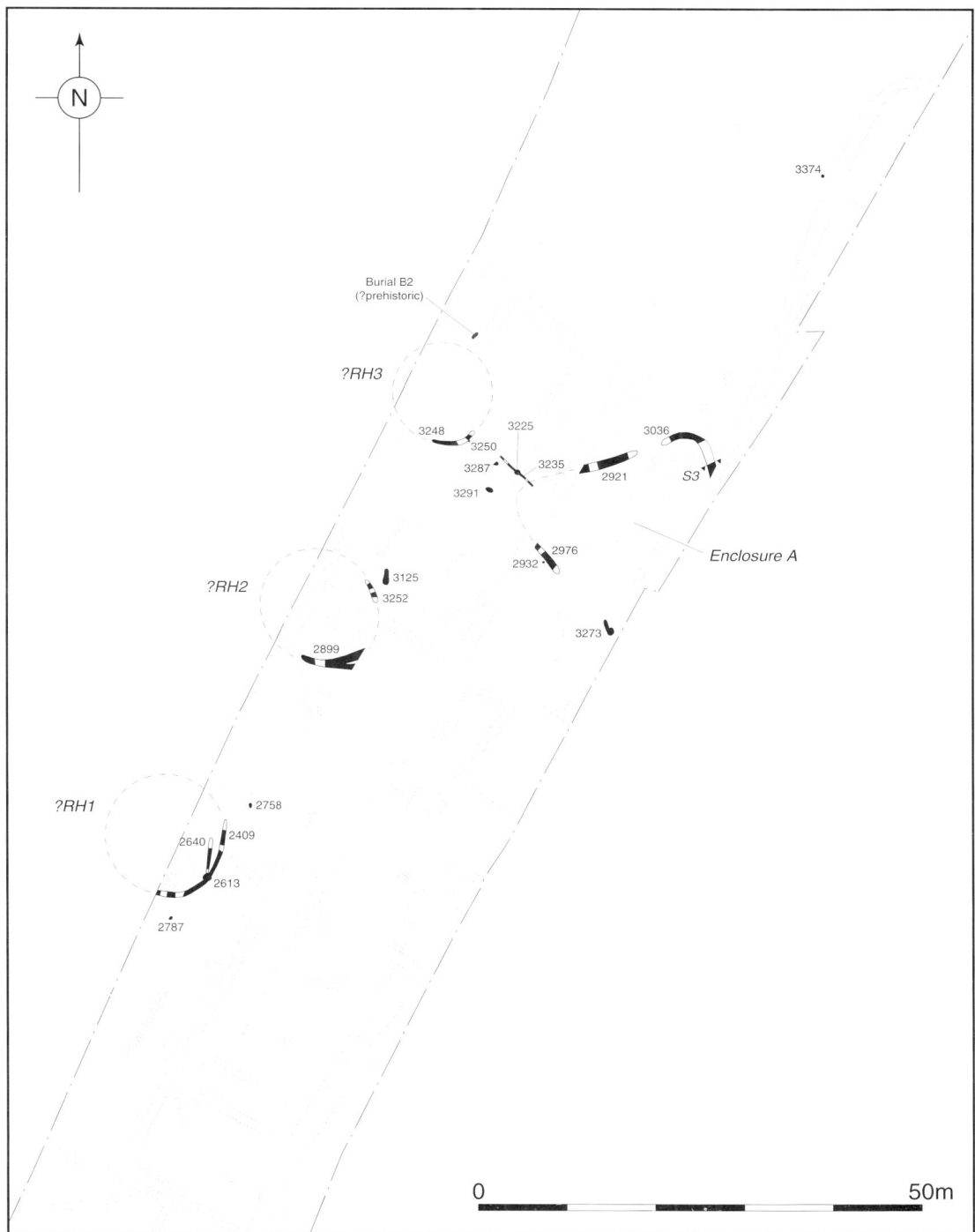

Fig. 6: Period 4.1 features (scale 1:750)

approximately 21m wide. Five undated postholes were found within the interior, although they are not necessarily contemporary with it. Lying on the projected alignment of the south-western boundary ditch was pit 3273, 90mm deep. This contained four sherds of handmade Malvernian and early Severn Valley ware pottery along with fragments of a non-ferrous crucible fragment, hearth lining and investment mould, the latter of Late Iron Age type.

To the north-west of Enclosure A was a narrow gully 3235, 4m long and 0.11m deep. Its relationship with the enclosure was not established although it cut across the projected alignment of the enclosure ditch. This gully was cut by 0.29m-deep pit 3225 which produced pottery of this period as did adjacent shallow pits 3287 and 3291 and, by the western edge of the enclosure, pit 2932. Some 33m north-east of Enclosure A, pit 3374 produced part of a Kingsholm fortress military-style flagon of pre-Flavian date amongst pottery of this period together with a Late Iron Age or Early Roman triangular loomweight fragment.

Assessment of the dating evidence
Approximately 150 sherds of handmade Malvernian and early Severn Valley wares were recovered from features assigned to this period. The largest assemblages were from pit 3374 (58 sherds), gully 2409 of ?RH1 (26 sherds), pit 3225 (16 sherds) and Enclosure A (10 sherds). Despite the small assemblage the pottery as a group can be dated broadly to the 1st and 2nd centuries AD. However, the occurrence of the pre-Flavian vessel, the triangular loomweight fragments and the pillar-moulded glass bowl implies a significant 1st-century element, particularly given the early 2nd-century date of Period 4.2.

Period 4.2: Early 2nd century AD (Fig. 7)
In the early 2nd century, a series of linear gullies and fencelines were established on the same alignment as Ermin Street to the south, although these were not all necessarily contemporary.

Four linear gullies on a north-east to south-west alignment were found. Gully 2369 was 0.42m deep and, to the south-west after a gap of 1.5m, its line was continued by 0.21m-deep gully 2426. Postholes 2547 and 2549 were found within the gap between these two gullies. Twenty metres to the west, parallel gully 2542 (also 0.21m deep) lay next to a shorter 0.11m-deep parallel gully 2544. To the north was shallow gully 2926. A further two gullies were aligned north-west to south-east: gully 2459 and, 14.2m further south, gully 2627. Just to the south-east of the latter's terminal were two postholes, 2622 and 2625.

Fenceline 1 consisted of 18 postholes between 0.08m and 0.23m deep and Fenceline 2 comprised 13 postholes and a shallow elongated gully. A kink in the fence alignment was mirrored by gully 2821. The relationship between the gullies and Fencelines 1 and 2 is uncertain. Approximately 27m to the north of Fenceline 2 was a parallel arrangement of nine irregularly spaced postholes (?Fenceline 3). No dating evidence was recovered from these and it is far from clear whether they formed a fence. The relationship of this possible boundary with a north-east/south-west-aligned linear posthole cluster along the western edge of the excavation was uncertain, although these may represent a series of fence boundaries. Again dating evidence from this cluster was limited with posthole 3137 producing three potsherds and posthole 2889 yielding tile, slag and triangular loomweight fragments. The relationship of these postholes with shallow curvilinear gully 3153 was not established although pottery of this period was recovered from the latter. Several other features produced pottery which can be assigned to the 2nd century AD: 0.14m-deep pit 2391, which was full of charcoal and burnt bone; pits 3216, 3269 and 2886; postholes 2987 and 2961 and gully 3143.

Fig. 7: Period 4.2 features (scale 1:750)

Assessment of the dating evidence
The pottery found in the features assigned to this period is dominated by Severn Valley and Dorset Black-Burnished (BB1) wares, with some Central Gaulish samian and Wiltshire grey wares. Approximately 260 sherds were recovered from the gullies, mostly from 2369 (163 sherds), with only a total of 30 sherds from Fencelines 1 and 2. The remaining features produced approximately 70 sherds. The assemblage suggests that this activity was taking place in the 2nd century AD, and given the early 2nd century date for the start of Period 4.3, Period 4.2 must have been relatively short-lived and contained within the first half of the 2nd century.

Period 4.3: 2nd to 4th centuries AD (Fig. 8)

During the earlier 2nd century there was a major reorganisation of the settlement layout with the establishment of ditched enclosures linked to Ermin Street by a 320m-long trackway. A small inhumation cemetery also dates to this period. The relationship between the cemetery and the Period 4.2 boundaries is uncertain and on ceramic grounds they could be contemporary. The cemetery has been assigned to this later phase as it was contained within an area defined by ditch 3283 immediately to the east and Enclosure C to the west, although it is conceivable that the Period 4.3 settlement was laid out so as to respect an existing cemetery. Pottery and coins indicate that the settlement continued in use until at least the early 4th century AD.

The cemetery
A roughly linear arrangement of 12 inhumations aligned north-south and north-east/south-west was found in the north-eastern part of the excavation area. One of the inhumations (Burial 13) cut through the boundary ditch of Period 4.1 Enclosure A, although there are no stratigraphic relationships with the Period 4.2 boundaries.

Grave catalogue
In the following catalogue, descriptions of the skeletons are by Tony Waldron, metalwork by Nina Crummy and animal bones by Tracey Stickler. Where finds are numbered, their location within the grave is marked on Fig. 9 and Figs 11 to 13.

INHUMATION BURIAL 3 (Fig. 9)
Grave: Plain subrectangular grave aligned south/north, measuring 1.87m x 0.66m x 0.16m, with coffin nails. The inhumation was supine. The left arm was raised level with the skull with the right arm bent over the abdomen. The right leg was fully extended and the left leg was bent with the left foot found near the right knee.
Skeleton: A young boy of between 15 and 25 at the time of death, and by far the most interesting skeleton in the group. The most striking feature of the skeleton was that the radius and ulna were substantially shorter than normal, being approximately 80% of their expected length. Similarly the right humerus was also about 80% of normal length, although the left was normal. Only the right tibia had survived, and although very badly damaged, was repaired sufficiently well to determine its length. It too was slightly shorter than normal. The boy thus had one of the so-called mesomelic dyschondroplasias, that is to say, the middle element of both limbs was shorter than normal.

The radii were also abnormally curved, and the distal articular surface was angled towards the ulna, whereas normally it is virtually straight. The abnormal curvature of the radius is referred to as Madelung's deformity, and it can be seen in the photograph of the skeleton taken *in situ* (Fig. 10). There are a number of systems of classification of the various entities; the type in which Madelung's deformity is associated with mesomelia is referred to as dyschondrosteosis (DCO; Langer 1965). The defect in DNA which results in this condition has recently been discovered, and it is now known that dyschondrosteosis is the heterozygous form of a much more severe type of mesomelia known as the Langer type (Berlin *et al.* 1998; Shers *et al.* 1998).

One of the features of DCO may be small stature, especially if the tibia is severely affected. However, unlike other forms of mesomelia, such as the Langer type, height is never greatly affected. In the present case, height was estimated to

Fig. 8: Period 4.3 features and anomalies from the geophysical surveys (scale 1:750)

Fig. 9: Burials 2, 3, 4, 6 and 7 (scale 1:20)

be 1.53m (about 5ft 2in) which is short, but not abnormally so. While he may not have been noticeably smaller than many of his contemporaries, there is no doubt that the deformity of his forearms would have been very obvious and would have impaired the mobility of his wrist.

All forms of mesomelia are rare, and although DCO is the most common type, it is seldom likely to be encountered in skeletal remains. Indeed, dwarfism of any variety is rare in the skeletal record, and there appears to be only a single other case of mesomelia in the palaeopathological literature, a skeleton dating to the Upper Palaeolithic in Italy. The height of this individual was estimated to have been between 1m and 1.3m and it was considered to be an example of acromesomelic dysplasia (Frayer *et al.* 1987). The present case may be the first of DCO to be found in human skeletal remains.

Finds: Nine iron nail shaft fragments from a wooden coffin.
1. Approximately 33 iron hobnails and fragments;
2. Approximately 81 iron hobnails and fragments. Average length 10mm.

The position of the hobnails indicates that the boy was buried wearing iron shod footware.

Pottery in the grave fill: 21 sherds, 2nd century AD.

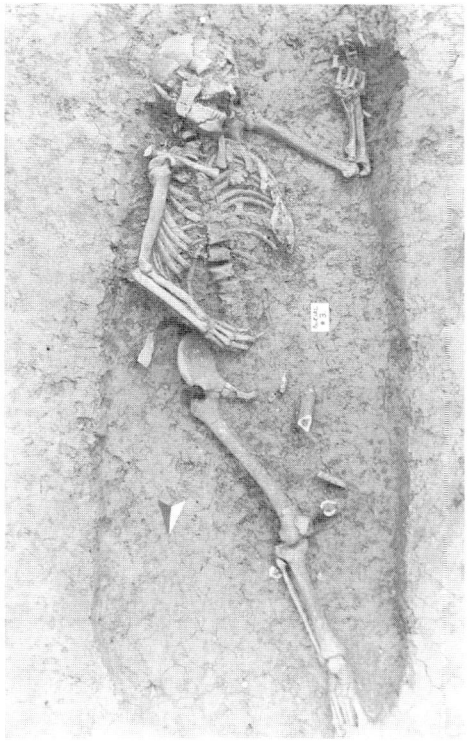

Fig. 10: Burial 3 as excavated

INHUMATION BURIAL 4 (Fig. 9)

Grave: Plain subrectangular grave aligned south-west/north-east measuring 1.55m x 0.6m x 0.12m. The inhumation was supine, with the legs flexed and the skull facing west. The left arm was placed over the chest and the right arm over the pelvis.

Skeleton: A female aged 35–45 at the time of death, this individual had osteoarthritis of the facet joints of the spine but was otherwise unremarkable. The skeleton had a large number of post-mortem breaks, and no long bone was sufficiently complete that measurements could be taken for an estimation of height.

Pottery in the grave fill: 7 sherds, 2nd century AD.

INHUMATION BURIAL 6 (Fig. 9)
Grave: Plain elongated oval-shaped grave aligned south/north, measuring 1.39m x 0.56m x 0.14m. The inhumation was supine with the legs flexed and the skull facing west. The left arm was extended by the side and the right arm bent across the abdomen.
Skeleton: A female aged at least 45 years when she died. She had osteoarthritis of the hands and spine, and probably also had an infection of the right wrist which had resulted in destruction of the normal integrity of some of the joints of the hand, especially the first to fourth carpo-metacarpal joints inclusive. In addition, the teeth of this skeleton displayed enamel hypoplasia, again indicative of some serious illness during childhood. Dental caries affected the left lower second premolar and the first molar. It was not possible to estimate the height of this individual because the long bones were either broken or incomplete.
Pottery in the grave fill: 12 sherds, 2nd century AD including Dorset BB1.

INHUMATION BURIAL 7 (Fig. 9)
Grave: Plain subrectangular grave aligned south-west/north-east, measuring 1.58m x 0.59m x 0.16m, with coffin nails. The inhumation was laid on its side facing west. Both arms were extended with the hands together and the legs were tightly flexed.
Skeleton: A female aged more than 45 years at death. She was 1.63m in height and had generalised osteoarthritis, the disease affecting her right hand, right elbow, right knee, right sterno-clavicular joint, spine and left hip. It is very likely that this woman would have been considerably incapacitated by her widespread disease, but it would not have been life threatening nor contributed to her death. Many teeth had been lost ante-mortem as the result of dental disease or gum disease, but none of those remaining had caries.
Finds: 18 iron nail shaft fragments and 10 Manning (1985) Type 1b nails (not all marked on the plan) from a wooden coffin.
Pottery in the grave fill: 38 sherds, 1st century AD.

INHUMATION BURIAL 9 (Fig. 11)
Grave: Plain subrectangular grave aligned north-east/south-west, measuring 1.14m x 0.6m x 0.2m, with coffin nails. The inhumation was supine with the legs tightly flexed and the skull bent down to face south-east. The right arm was bent towards the jaw with the left arm extended.
Skeleton: A female, 45 years or older, and only 1.53m in height. She had osteoarthritis affecting her right hand and right sterno-clavicular joint. She also had degenerative disc disease affecting her three lower lumbar vertebrae, marginal osteophytes on all her lumbar vertebra, and Schmorl's nodes and marginal osteophytes on the five lowest thoracic vertebrae. Disc degeneration is a common, age-related phenomenon and may be associated with back pain, particularly if a prolapsed disc or large marginal osteophytes impinge upon one of the spinal nerves as they leave the spine through the inter-vertebral foramina. Whether this was the case in this individual it is impossible to say. The Schmorl's nodes, which are due to pressure caused by the herniation of the central part of the inter-vertebral disc through the outer fibrous part, are very commonly seen in skeletal material and generally cause no symptoms during life.

Both lower first incisors had been lost during life, perhaps as the result of trauma, although primary dental disease or gum disease cannot be ruled out as causes. None of the extant teeth had caries.

The first and third metacarpals of the right hand were stained green, as was the first proximal phalanx and the hamate, due to leaching of copper salts from a copper-alloy armlet buried with the body.
Finds: 17 iron nail shaft fragments, 4 nail heads and 11 Manning (1985) Type 1b nails (not all marked on the plan) from a wooden coffin.
1. Copper-alloy penannular armlet found on the right wrist (Fig. 11.1). Plain but well-formed snake's-head terminals. Maximum internal diameter 56.5mm. Rounded upright section, height 6.5mm, 4mm thick;
2. (n.i.) Iron strip fragment. Length 39mm, 8mm wide, 1.5mm thick.
Pottery in the grave fill: 36 sherds, early 2nd century AD including Dorset BB1.

INHUMATION BURIAL 10 (n.i.)
Grave: Heavily plough-damaged grave aligned north-east/south-west, measuring 0.6m x 0.2m x 0.02m.
Skeleton: Fragmentary, consisting of little more than some fragments of the right distal humerus and ulna and several unidentified fragments. Adult, but neither age nor sex could be determined.

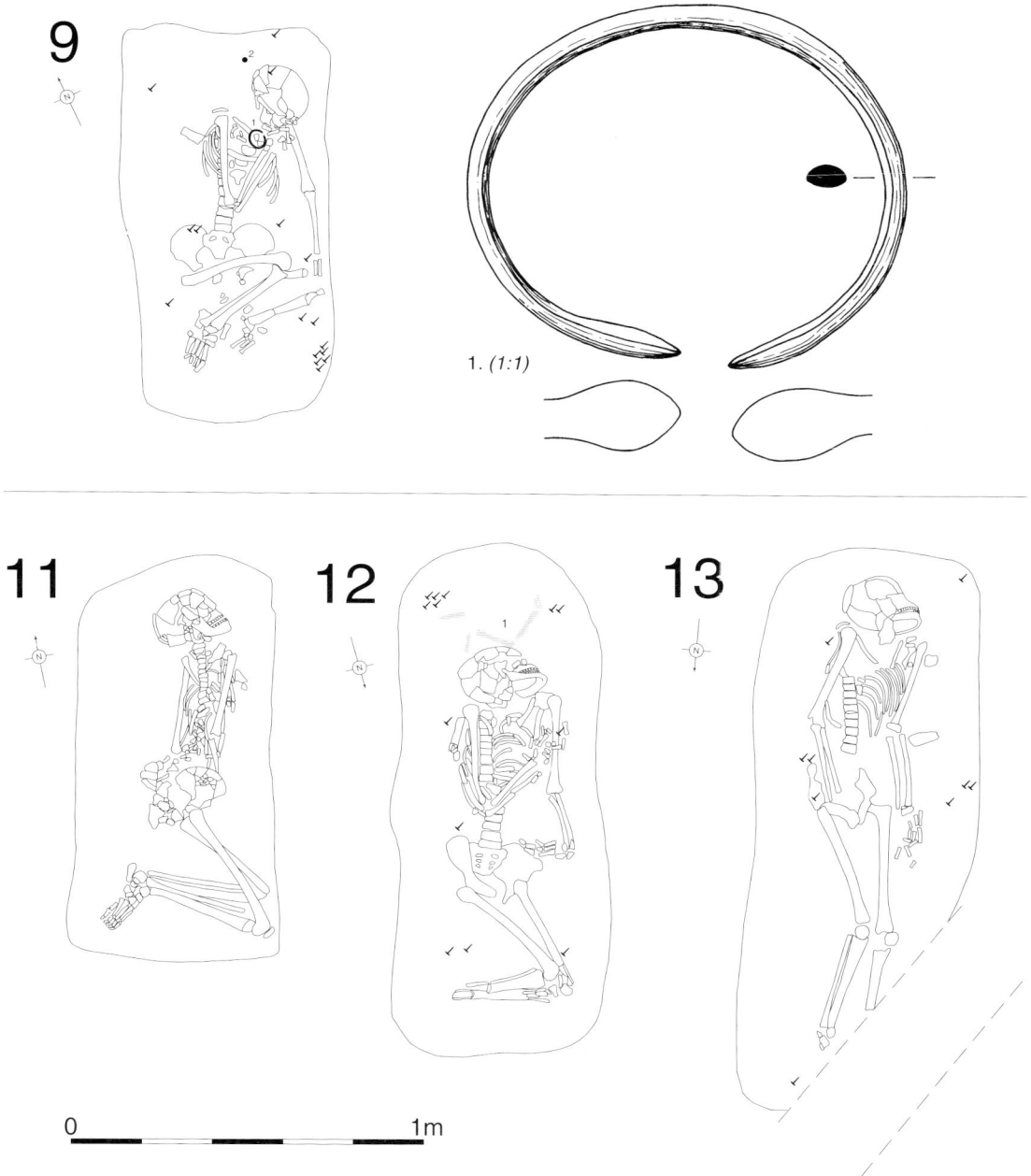

Fig. 11: Burials 9, 11, 12 and 13 (scale 1:20)

INHUMATION BURIAL 11 (Fig. 11)
Grave: Plain subrectangular grave aligned north/south, measuring 1.18m x 0.6m x 0.18m. The inhumation was laid on its side with the skull facing east. The right arm was by the side and the left arm bent with the hand beneath the neck. Both legs were tightly flexed.
Skeleton: A female aged between 25 and 35 at death and 1.59m in height, this skeleton was virtually complete. There was some non-specific periostitis on the shafts of both femurs and tibiae and degenerative disc disease between the fifth lumbar vertebra and first sacral segments.
Pottery in the grave fill: Seven sherds, ?2nd century AD.

INHUMATION BURIAL 12 (Fig. 11)
Grave: Plain subrectangular grave aligned south-west/north-east, measuring 1.5m x 0.6m x 0.15m, with coffin nails. The inhumation was supine with the legs flexed and the skull facing west. The left arm was extended by the side and the right arm was bent to cross the chest.
Skeleton: A female between 15 and 25 years of age. Height could not be estimated because all the long bones had post-mortem breaks. The skeleton had no pathology apart from caries affecting the left lower first molar.
Finds: Nine iron nail shaft fragments and five Manning (1985) Type 1b nails from a wooden coffin.
1. An uncooked articulated leg of lamb above the skull.

INHUMATION BURIAL 13 (Fig. 11)
Grave: Plain irregular subrectangular grave aligned south/north, measuring 1.65m x 0.64m x 0.15m, with coffin nails. The inhumation was supine with arms and legs extended and the skull facing west.
Skeleton: Female aged at least 45 years and 1.59m in height. She had osteoarthritis of the right elbow, both hands and both wrists. Three teeth were affected by dental caries: the left upper first and second molars and the right upper second molar.
Finds: Three iron nail shaft fragments and seven Manning (1985) Type 1b nails (not all marked on the plan) from a wooden coffin.
Pottery in the grave fill: 26 sherds, 1st to 2nd century AD.

INHUMATION BURIAL 14 (Fig. 12)
Grave: Plain subrectangular grave aligned south-west/north-east, measuring 1.47m x 0.6m x 0.15m, with coffin nails. The inhumation was laid on its side with the skull facing north-west. The right arm was bent by the side of the jaw and the left arm extended. Most of both legs did not survive but the position of the left foot suggests that they were flexed.
Skeleton: This was the only other positively identified male in the group, but the skeleton was very fragmentary, and the extant bones broken, so neither age nor height could be determined. No fewer than 11 of the teeth in the mandible had been lost during life which suggests that this individual had severe gum disease. He also had degenerative disc disease affecting the three lower cervical vertebrae. This is often a cause of pain in the shoulders and arms in modern clinical practice, and this individual may well have suffered likewise.
Finds: Seven iron nail shaft fragments from a wooden coffin.
1. Iron strap with a nail fixed through it. Length of nail 36mm; length of strap (incomplete) 41mm, width 32mm.
Pottery in the grave fill: 5 sherds, ?1st century AD.

INHUMATION BURIAL 15 (Fig. 12)
Grave: Plain subrectangular grave aligned north-east/south-west, measuring 1.58m x 0.94m x 0.27m. The inhumation was supine with the legs tightly flexed. The arms were crossed over the chest and the skull faced south-west and rested on the left shoulder.
Skeleton: Female aged between 15 and 25. The long bones had all suffered post-mortem damage and an estimate of height could not be made; no pathological changes were noted in either the bones or the teeth.
Finds: Ten iron nail shaft fragments and two Manning (1985) Type 1b nails, possibly from the box described below.
Iron fittings from a box.
1. Drop-handle with a wide flat section, the ends narrowing to a square section and curled outwards. One end is damaged. Small fragments of the double-spiked loops used to fix the handle to the wood remain in the centre of each loop. Length (incomplete) 99mm, depth 54mm;
2. Fitting for the bolt with wide flanges on either side of a flat-based central section. Maximum surviving length 86mm, width 82mm;
3. Fragments of iron sheet from the lock. Very little remains of the original edges. Maximum dimensions: 84 by 75mm; 104 by 48mm; 74 by 51mm; 42 by 26mm; 35 by 25mm (n.i.);

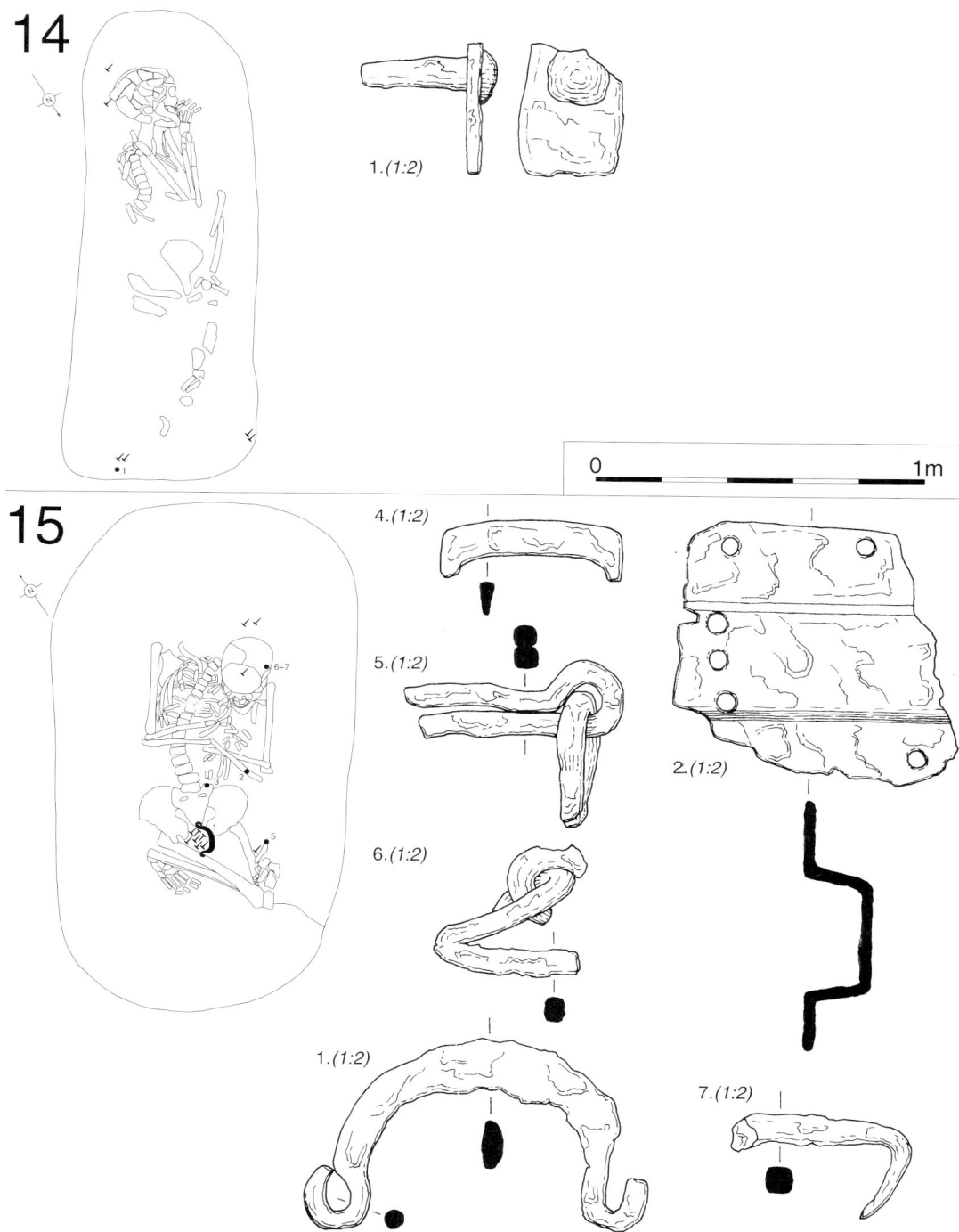

Fig. 12: Burials 14 and 15 (scale 1:20)

4. Cramp or joiner's dog with short returned ends, the tips missing. Width 57mm, length 16mm (location not marked on the plan);
5. Hinge formed from a pair of linked double-spiked loops. The ends of the spikes are missing. At about 13mm, the square-section spikes are very stout. The length of the best-preserved spike is 65mm;
6. Fragment of a double-spiked loop or ring-headed pin. The rectangular-section shaft is bent at a sharp angle. Approximate length if straight 109mm;
7. Four shaft fragments, of which one is illustrated. The longest is square in section at the top, hammered to a flat point at the tip, which is clenched. Probably from a nail or double-spiked loop. Length (bent) 56mm. Of the three short pieces, two have a square section, one a rectangular section. The latter may belong to item 6.
Pottery in the grave fill: 24 sherds, broadly 2nd century AD including Dorset BB1.

INHUMATION BURIAL 16 (Fig. 13)
Grave: Plain subrectangular grave aligned south-west/north-east, measuring 2.16m x 0.65m x 0.22m. The inhumation was supine with the legs extended. The left arm was slightly bent over the pelvis and the right arm crossed the abdomen.
Skeleton: Female of at least 45 years. She survived only as a partial skeleton with considerable post-mortem damage. Only three of the lumbar vertebrae had survived but all were affected by degenerative disc disease; there were no other pathological changes.
Finds: Two iron nail shaft fragments.
1. Complete copper-alloy trumpet brooch of the late 1st or early 2nd century AD. The head-loop rises from a small rectangular plate on the head. The spring is held between two large lugs. The acanthus button is frontal only, with upper and lower mouldings. The foot is cruciform in section, with the back rib flaring out to form the solid catchplate. The foot-knob has two mouldings. Length 57mm;
2. Twenty-two iron hobnails, including six corroded together in two groups of three. Average length 10mm. The position of the hobnails indicates burial with iron shod footware;
3. Three hobnails.
Pottery in the grave fill: 23 sherds, 1st to 2nd century including Central Gaulish samian ware.

Assessment of the date of the cemetery

The grave goods from Burials 9, 15 and 16 probably date within the Trajanic to Antonine periods, while the rite of depositing shoes with a corpse (Burials 3 and 16) was long-lived. Over 180 sherds of pottery were deposited incidentally within the grave fills, consisting principally of Severn Valley, Dorset Black-Burnished and Malvernian wares but with a component of early Severn Valley and Savernake grog-tempered wares from Burials 7, 9, 13, 14 and 16. Taken together, the evidence suggests that the cemetery was in use in the first half of the 2nd century AD.

The settlement (Fig. 8)

The cemetery appears to have been contained within an area defined to the north-west by Enclosure C and to the south-east by ditch 3283. The geophysical survey (Fig. 2) indicates dense settlement activity to the west of the excavation area while to the south-east the anomalies are more suggestive of fields and paddocks abutting the main trackway that provided access to Ermin Street.

THE NORTH-EASTERN PART OF THE SETTLEMENT (2nd to later 3rd/early 4th century AD)
Ditch 3283 was 0.43m deep and as it ran north-eastwards beyond Enclosure C its course became unclear, as the ditch fills were virtually identical to the alluvium through which it was cut. However, at its northern limit traces of a south-eastern turn were identified within which was a large 0.3m-deep depression 3386, the fills of which were also alluvial in character (Fig. 3). The function of this depression is uncertain although it may have been receiving water run-off in an area of increasingly marshy ground adjacent to the Horsbere Brook. Ditch 3283 can be traced south-westwards beyond the excavated area as a clear anomaly on the geophysical survey, before re-entering the excavation area as ditch 2744/2494. Ditch 3283 was partially recut along the same alignment by a 0.4m-deep ditch 3042 with a north-eastern terminal.

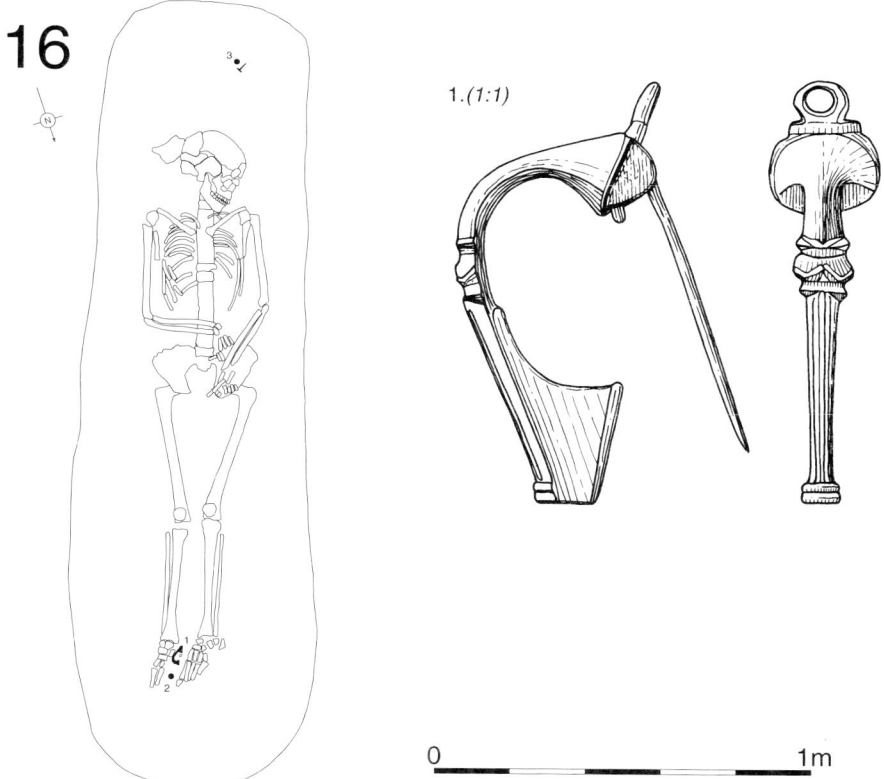

Fig. 13: Burial 16 (scale 1:20)

MIDDEN

Contained within the area defined by ditch 3283 was pit 2848 which, within the excavation area, covered an area of 12m x 11m. It was typically 0.4m deep (Fig. 14, section 7). It contained three fills and the loose black silty clay consistency of the final and major fill 2849 suggests that, in its final phase at least, it was used as a midden. The grave of a terrier-sized dog was found within the midden and several postholes along its boundary probably formed a boundary fence. The midden was cut by a shallow L-shaped gully 2973 of uncertain function.

ENCLOSURE C

Cutting through the boundary ditches of Period 4.1 Enclosure A was the boundary ditch 3053 of Enclosure C, three sides of which were found within the excavation area. The location of the fourth side can be reliably inferred from the geophysical survey, giving total dimensions of 40m by 26m. The enclosure respected the western extent of the cemetery, and its ditch had been recut at least once (Fig. 14, section 4). Internally it contained several features including a curvilinear gully 3151, and a crouched burial (Burial 2) for which a prehistoric date may be most appropriate (see above).

THE SOUTH-WESTERN PART OF THE SETTLEMENT (2nd to later 3rd/earlier 4th century AD)

THE DITCHED TRACKWAY AND ENCLOSURE B

Cutting Period 4.2 gullies 2369 and 2426 was north-east/south-west-aligned linear ditch 2199 which ran for a length of 195m from Ermin Street before turning to the west and finally south to define three sides of Enclosure B. The ditch defined the north-western side of a trackway while its opposite side is mostly known from geophysics, although a portion of it was examined at the southern end of the excavation area as ditch 2203 where the track proved to be 13m wide (Fig. 3). Ditch 2199 (Fig. 14, section 1) was typically 1.75m wide and 0.85m deep and had been recut at least once. There was no indication of any associated bank.

Structure 6 was contained within, and may be contemporary with, Enclosure B. It was represented by three large stone-packed postholes 2430, 2435, 2651. Posthole 2430 was 0.6m in diameter and 0.75m deep; posthole 2435 was 0.9m in diameter and 0.63m deep; and posthole 2651 was 1.2m in diameter and 0.3m deep (Fig. 14, section 2). To the south, smaller postholes 2642 and 2644 may represent a south-western continuation of the structure. The relationship between Structure 6 and two shallow gullies 2678 and 2531 on the supposed alignment of the structure was not established. A few other features within the bounds of Enclosure B also produced sherds current in the 2nd and 3rd centuries AD, including pit 2465 and three of a cluster of four intercutting pits 2664, 2665 and 2666.

ENCLOSURE D

Enclosure D was constructed immediately to the north-west of the trackway and to the south-west of Enclosure B. The fact that the trackway ditch was not used for its eastern arm may suggest that, although the trackway could still have been in use, it had largely silted up requiring the construction of another ditch 2416 for the enclosure. The juxtaposition of the two ditches implies that the track did not have an external bank beyond the outer lip of the ditch (Fig. 14, section 1). The south-western arm of the enclosure had been removed by later ditch 2365, while the north-west side can probably be identified in the geophysical survey (Fig. 3), in which case Enclosure D had approximate dimensions of 27m by 33m. Enclosure ditch 2416 was 0.53m deep and had been recut at least once. The interior was divided into two by a 0.25m-deep internal ditch 2600. Internal features included two shallow gullies 2359 and 2631 and possibly gully 2294 as well.

LATER DEVELOPMENTS (late 3rd to early 4th century AD)

In this section a variety of features which are either stratigraphically later than the features discussed above, or else produced some of the latest artefacts from the site, are discussed.

The ditches of Enclosures B and D appear to have been filled in by the middle of the 3rd century AD, when replanning of the south-western part of the settlement occurred. Enclosure E was constructed, while the south-western side of Enclosure D was replaced by a series of recut ditches 2365 on the same alignment. These developments may have occurred while Enclosure C was still functioning, although the latter was in turn cut by ditch 2985.

ENCLOSURE E AND DITCH 2365

Cutting the north-western side of Enclosure B was the 0.37m-deep boundary ditch of Enclosure E (Fig. 14, section 5). The relationship between 2368 and ditch 2416 defining the north-east side of Enclosure D could not be ascertained. A gap, presumably for an entrance was apparent on its north-eastern side while the south-western side had been removed by a later ditch. Outside of the

Section 1. *Trackway and enclosure D*

Section 2. *Structure 6 posthole*

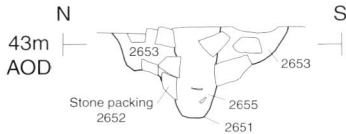

Section 3. *Enclosure A*   **Section 4.** *Enclosure C*   **Section 5.** *Enclosure E*

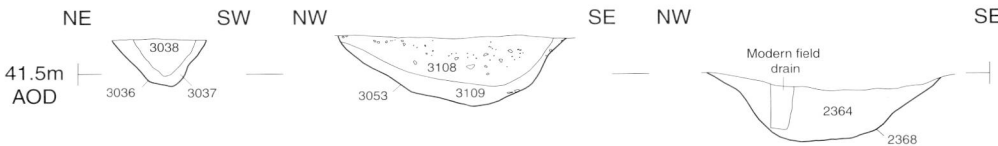

Section 6. *Ditch 2365*

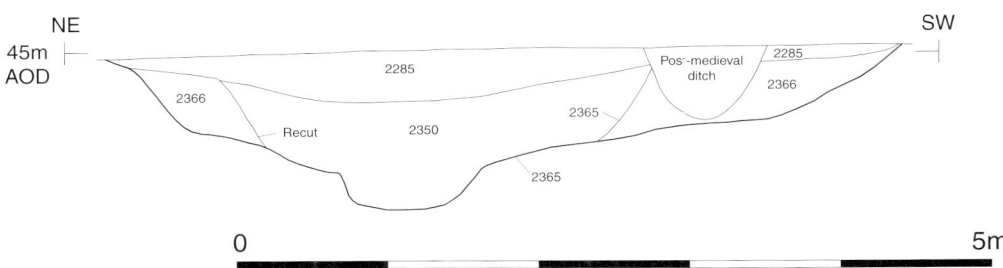

Section 7. *Midden*

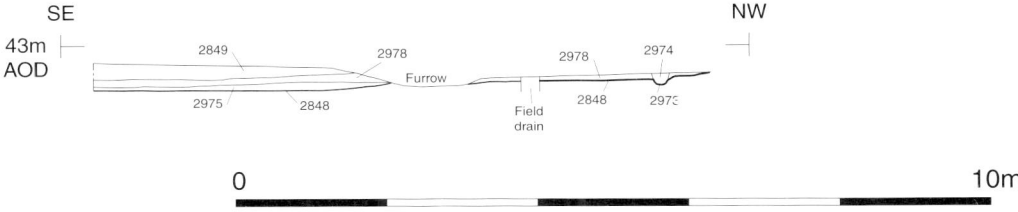

Fig. 14: Sections (1-6 scale 1:50; 7 scale 1:100)

enclosure the terminals of gully 2414 appeared to respect its eastern boundary. Ditch 2365 demarcated the southern limit of the settlement and cut through a number of earlier ditches which probably formed the southern arms of Enclosures D and E. The ditch turned to the north-east to respect the trackway.

DITCH 2985
Cutting the south-western boundary ditch of Enclosure C was a 0.6m-deep curvilinear ditch 2985, most of which lay beyond the excavation area. There was a 0.35m-wide and 0.2m-deep gully 3147 with stone-lined sides on the western side of the ditch, as well as and two other gullies (3110, 3113). A further stone-lined gully 3232 was found just to the north of ditch 2985. A possible gravel surface 3155 (n.i.), 50mm thick, lay to the north-east of gully 3147.

THE TRACKWAY
Only a few of the sections cut across trackway ditch 2199 produced evidence for recutting, although a coin of AD 367–75 was found in the primary fill (3321) of one of these recuts. The trackway ditch was therefore probably still a visible landmark into the later 4th century.

Assessment of the dating evidence
Given the overwhelming preponderance of Severn Valley and Dorset Black-Burnished wares found in the features it is difficult to provide a clear chronological framework for the development of the site during the 2nd to 4th centuries. Indeed, the relationship between the cemetery and the Period 4.2 boundaries is uncertain and they could on ceramic grounds be contemporary. The cemetery appears to date to the first half of the 2nd century, and the main boundary ditch 3283 (and recut 3042) contained similar wares to those found in the grave fillings, albeit without the earlier component.

The midden 2848 yielded an assemblage of 776 sherds consisting mainly of Dorset Black-Burnished and Severn Valley wares but also with micaceous greywares which first appear in the late 2nd century, and a sherd of Oxfordshire whiteware mortaria. A greater variety of imports such as Dressel 20 amphora, samian and North Gaulish mortaria are also present. Overall the pottery suggests that the midden accumulated in the first half of the 3rd century AD.

The ditch of Enclosure C was recut at least once, although no differentiation could be established between the pottery in the original fills and that in the recut. The ditch contained over 300 potsherds. Once again, 2nd-century wares predominate but with a small component of late 2nd to 3rd-century micaceous greywares, 3rd or 4th-century Oxfordshire wares including colour-coated sherds, and a 3rd or 4th-century Dorset Black-Burnished ware cooking-pot sherd with oblique lattice. This suggests that the enclosure was established during the 2nd century AD and that the ditches continued to accumulate material until at least the mid 3rd century, and perhaps as late as the early 4th century AD. Gully 3151 within Enclosure C contained wares current in the 2nd to 3rd century.

In the south-western part of the settlement a coin dating to AD 117–38 was found within primary fill 2852 of trackway ditch 2199, while the ditch yielded an assemblage of approximately 290 potsherds. The majority of these date to the 2nd century, but with a small component of micaceous greywares which appear in the late 2nd or early 3rd century; a sherd of Oxfordshire whiteware mortaria (Young type M13/14) dated to AD 180–240, and a 3rd or 4th-century sherd of Dorset Black-Burnished ware cooking pot with oblique lattice. Pit 2387 adjacent to the terminal also produced wares current in the 2nd century AD as did small gully offshoots 2537 and 2841, and posthole 2740 to the south of the terminal. The ditch of Enclosure B therefore appears to have remained at least partly open into the middle of the 3rd century AD.

A total of 60 sherds was recovered from the postholes of Structure 6, consisting mainly of Dorset Black-Burnished and Severn Valley wares. Combined with the lack of micaceous greywares, this suggests a 2nd-century construction date. Sherds of micaceous greyware and Oxfordshire colour coat found in the postpipe of 2651 suggest a later 3rd or early 4th-century demolition date, as does a coin of AD 260–8 found in the postpipe of 2435.

The ditch of Enclosure D yielded a total of 124 sherds, again dominated by Severn Valley and Dorset Black-Burnished wares with some micaceous greywares and one sherd of South West White-Slipped ware which first appears in the later 2nd century. This ditch therefore seems to have been filled by the earlier 3rd century.

The ditch fills of Enclosure E produced over 200 sherds, again dominated by Severn Valley and Dorset Black-Burnished wares, but with micaceous greywares (16), Oxfordshire colour coat (1) and whiteware mortaria (2), and Black-Burnished ware cooking pots with obtuse lattice decoration (16), suggesting that the ditch remained open until the late 3rd or early 4th century. Pottery from gully 2414 included micaceous greywares. Ditch 2365 contained fewer sherds of micaceous greyware than Enclosures D and E, but produced sherds of Oxfordshire colour coat and Oxfordshire Parchment ware which were current in the mid to late 3rd to 4th centuries. A coin of AD 273–4 was found in the uppermost fill (3329) of one of the sections cut through this ditch. Gully 2294 also produced wares current in the 3rd to 4th century AD.

The fill of ditch 2985 produced over 90 sherds, again with Dorset Black-Burnished and Severn Valley wares, although including micaceous greywares and part of a Dorset Black-Burnished conical flanged bowl which was current from the mid to late 3rd century onwards.

On balance it would appear that the majority of features on the site had fallen out of use by the end of the 3rd or beginning of the 4th century, with fills of Enclosures C and E and ditch 2365 producing material of this date. Ditch 2985 which cuts Enclosure C probably dates to the 4th century, although the majority of this feature lay outside of the excavated area. Trackway ditch 2199 displayed evidence for recutting in some places, and the fill of one such recut produced a coin of AD 367–75 which indicates that it was still a visible landscape feature into the later 4th century. An unstratified coin of AD 313–14 and another of AD 330–40 found in a medieval plough furrow further testify to continued activity of some description in the vicinity of the excavated area in the 4th century.

Period 5: medieval agriculture (Fig. 3)

Evidence for medieval activity was restricted to three separate ridge and furrow field systems that correspond with the field pattern depicted on the 1842 Churchdown Tithe Map. Within the central area of the site the ridge and furrow was broadly parallel with the main alignment of the Romano-British trackway and enclosures (Fig. 3). This suggests that the earthworks of the Romano-British settlement and its field systems survived long enough to influence the basic alignments of medieval agricultural activity.

THE RADIOCARBON DATES

Five samples from three features were submitted to the Scottish Universities Research and Reactor Centre for radiocarbon dating: two from Cremation 1 (2240); one from fill 2166 of posthole 2165 of Structure 1, and two from the fill 2223 of pit 2224 that lay within that structure. Calibrated age ranges were determined from the University of Washington Quaternary Isotope Laboratory Dating Program, Rev. 4.0 1998. The results are listed in Table 1.

Table 1: Radiocarbon determinations

Laboratory no.	Context	Material	Radiocarbon Age BP	Calibrated 2σ 95.4% confidence
AA-33587 (GU-8272)	2166	Oak charcoal	2450 ± 50	787-399 cal. BC
AA-33586 (GU-8273)	2223	Charred seed (Avena sp.)	2390 ± 50	760-385 cal. BC
AA-33585 (GU-8274)	2223	Oak twigs charcoal	2375 ± 60	761-262 cal. BC
AA-33584 (GU-8275)	2240	Charred seeds (Hawthorn)	3040 ± 50	1413-1128 cal. BC
AA-33583 (GU-8276)	2240	Charred tuber (Arrhenatherum elatius)	2965 ± 60	1388-1000 cal. BC

THE FINDS

The Pottery, by Jane Timby with a contribution from Alan Vince

An assemblage of 5578 sherds of pottery weighing 51 kg was recovered. Most of the material dates to the Roman period but small amounts of prehistoric, medieval and post-medieval wares are also present. The pottery was recovered from 348 individual contexts. Of these around 66% yielded ten or fewer sherds which clearly has some impact on the reliability of the dating in many cases. The condition of the material varied greatly, the prehistoric sherds being particularly degraded. The Roman wares, although better preserved, are still quite broken-up, suggestive of material that has been subjected to ongoing disturbance or surface exposure. The juxtaposition of material of different dates in various features indicates quite a high level of redeposition across the site.

The assemblage was sorted into fabrics based on the type, size and frequency of the macroscopically visible inclusions in the pastes. The prehistoric material was analysed following the guidelines set out in PCRG 1992. The Roman traded wares are coded according to the recommended nomenclature set out in the National Roman Fabric Reference Collection (NRFRC; Tomber and Dore 1998). Local and other regional wares are coded using a similar system of coding to the NRFRC but are specific to the Gloucestershire area. All the material was quantified by sherd count, weight and rim estimated vessel equivalence (EVE), for each excavated context. The data were put onto a spreadsheet, a copy of which is deposited with the site archive.

In the following report the prehistoric material is discussed first, followed by the Roman. The medieval and post-medieval material is negligible in quantity and not discussed in detail.

Prehistoric

Approximately 256 sherds (1676g) were designated as prehistoric. This excludes later Iron Age native wares, in particular Malvernian wares and grog-tempered wares, which persist into the Roman period, unless those sherds occurred in prehistoric contexts. Certain fabrics, notably the Malvernian wares, have quite a long currency from the Middle Iron Age through to the 2nd century AD and it is thus difficult to be certain about the dates without accompanying material. By the same token the use of a thick-walled grog-tempered fabric for storage jars from the early 1st century AD in the area caused some problems in discriminating this from potential Bronze Age urn when the sherds occurred in Roman contexts. If these other native-style wares are added the 'prehistoric' total amounts to 486 sherds (2468g).

The prehistoric material is exceptionally abraded. The average sherd size at 6.5g to a certain extent reflects this, but the presence of some quite large urn fragments slightly skews the figure, which is smaller for much of the material. Many fragments were too small and rounded even to be certain they were pottery and not fired clay. There are almost no rim sherds or other featured sherds other than base sherds. Dating of the prehistoric sherds, therefore, can only be regarded as quite provisional. There is very little comparative material, particularly for the Bronze Age, from the locality.

The sherds have been grouped together as wares based on the main fabric constituents, although in reality there was enormous variety across the group indicating small sherds from a large number of vessels with potentially a wide chronological range. Table 2 quantifies the fabrics according to the phasing sequence.

Table 2: Prehistoric fabrics by period
  Weight (Wt) is in grammes

Fabric	Description	Quantity by period					
		2 No.	2 Wt	3 No.	3 Wt	4-5 No.	4-5 Wt
GROG1	fine fabric, grog	0	0	0	0	1	2
GROG2	soapy grog-tempered	1	70	1	4	14	152
FLGR	flint-tempered with grog	0	0	1	15	0	0
GRCALC	grog with limestone	22	162	1	2	0	0
ROCK	doleritic	75	660	1	5	0	0
CALC1	fossil shell and limestone	0	0	23	115	23	76
CALC2	micaceous with limestone	0	0	1	1	1	1
CALC3	limestone with occasional iron	0	0	3	21	0	0
CALC4	limestone with quartz sand	0	0	1	9	2	27
CALC5	very vesicular, leached limestone	0	0	2	4	1	4
CALC6	mainly oolitic limestone	0	0	11	9	7	15
GRSAND	sandy with grog	0	0	0	0	1	57
SAND1	very micaceous, fine silty	0	0	5	8	2	3
SAND2	dense medium sandy	0	0	14	22	3	12
SAND3	ill-sorted sand, rare limestone	0	0	2	8	1	3
SAND4	fine sandy	0	0	0	0	3	27
MAL REA	Malvernian rock-tempered	0	0	7	3	0	0
MAL LI	Malverian limestone	0	0	0	0	0	0
unid	too small to identify	0	0	2	3	0	0
SVW EA	early Severn Valley ware	0	0	2	10	0	0
Total		98	892	75	229	59	379

Prehistoric fabrics

BEAKER
GROG1: Orange-red exterior with a black core. The paste contains a moderate frequency of ill-sorted, sub-angular, light orange-coloured grog; larger fragments up to 3mm across. Smooth soapy feel.

MIDDLE BRONZE AGE
ROCK, by Alan Vince: Visually, the fabric is characterised by angular fragments of a dark crystalline rock ranging up to 10mm across. All these rock fragments had a similar colour and texture and have the appearance of deliberately crushed and added temper. The groundmass consists of inclusionless clay.

In thin-section (sample V360) only one fragment of the dark rock was present. This was an angular fragment of fine-grained basic igneous rock, 1mm across, composed of laths of feldspar and chlorite with minor magnetite. Other inclusions consisted of sparse rounded quartzose sand, composed of quartz and fine-grained sandstone (grains up to 0.2mm) fragments up to 0.4mm across, sparse rounded red iron-rich compound and rounded fragments of relict clay of varying colour and texture. These range from inclusionless light-coloured clays to quartz sand-tempered dark brown pellets. It is possible that the latter are grog, although if so they were sufficiently soft to become rounded during clay preparation. The groundmass consists of inclusionless high birefringent clay with patterned extinction and sparse laths of muscovite.

The clay matrix and light-coloured clay pellets are consistent with the use of a Jurassic clay, such as the Lower Lias or Oxford clays. There is insufficient muscovite present for the Middle or Upper Lias clays. There are too few sand grains present to characterise the quartzose sand. The rounding and size is consistent with sands found in the Severn Valley rather than further north or north-east where the sands tend to contain high quantities of sandstone-derived grains with euhedral overgrowth.

The red clay pellets and the basic igneous rock are inconsistent with a local origin. Basic igneous rock fragments are a commonplace tempering material in Bronze Age and Iron Age pottery in the highland zone, being found in the Welsh borderland, the Peak District, the Lindsey Marshes on the Lincolnshire coast and extensively north of the Humber. When compared with thin sections of two basic igneous rock-tempered sherds from Kexby, North Yorkshire, the Gloucestershire sherd contains few inclusions and the character of the quartzose sand is different (the Kexby sand is coarser textured and contains coarse grained sandstone fragments).

On the basis of the available petrological information, the vessel could have been produced locally in Gloucestershire and tempered with crushed exotic rock, obtained either from boulder clay or direct from the outcrop, for example, in the Derbyshire Peaks. Alternatively, the vessel may itself be an import from the north, although the character of the groundmass argues against this. Although chemical analysis of the clay was obtained, no suitable local comparanda (analyses of Jurassic clays) are available at present.

GROG2: Generally oxidised surfaces, occasionally black, with a grey-black core. The slightly micaceous paste has a smooth, slightly soapy feel and contains a moderate frequency of mainly light-coloured, sub-angular crushed grog fragments up to 2 to 3mm in size. Sherds are generally around 12 to 14mm thick.

FLGR: A finely micaceous, slightly gritty fabric. The paste contains a sparse scatter of fine rounded quartz sand visible at x20 magnification, rare inclusions of angular flint, ironstone and light-coloured grog, all up to 2mm in size. Dark orange-brown surfaces with a grey core.

GRCALC: Soft fabric containing a common frequency of calcareous inclusions comprising oolitic limestone, limestone fragments and fossiliferous matter visible only in fresh fracture. Larger fragments up to 2mm, mainly finer. On the surfaces these inclusions have decayed leaving voids. The paste also contains a sparse frequency of sub-angular grog. Poorly consolidated clay matrix. Orange surfaces with a grey core.

GRSAND: Fabric as GROG2 but with a scatter of fine, rounded, well-sorted quartz sand.

MID-LATE BRONZE AGE/EARLY IRON AGE

CALC1: A mainly oxidised ware, occasionally with a darker brown interior surface. The fabric has a smooth, greasy feel with occasional surface voids. In fresh fracture the paste contains a moderate to common density of decaying calcareous inclusions, limestone and fossiliferous material, larger fragments up to 3mm across. Generally thick-walled vessels, 12 to 15mm across.

CALC2: Very small sherds characterised by a highly micaceous paste containing a sparse to moderate frequency of oolitic limestone.

CALC3: A moderately hard, mainly oxidised fabric as CALC4 containing limestone/voids and quartz sand but with occasional rounded dark red-brown ferruginous inclusions up to 1 to 2mm in size.

CALC4: A moderately hard, largely oxidised ware similar to CALC1 but with a slightly rough surface feel. The paste contains a scatter of moderately well-sorted, rounded quartz sand in addition to the voids/calcareous inclusions.

CALC5: Sherds. dark and light orange through to black in colour with an extremely vesicular texture. The voids, varying from fine up to 3 to 4mm across, have been left from leached calcareous material leaving a friable, very light fabric.

CALC6: Brown or grey ware with a brown core with orange-red margins. The paste contains a sparse to common frequency of discrete grains of oolitic limestone accompanied by fine fossiliferous material.

SAND1: A highly micaceous, fine ware with a silty texture, grey or red-brown in colour. Quite soft, most sherds being very abraded. Variable quantities of fine sand.

SAND2: A reddish-brown exterior with a black core and interior surface. A moderately hard ware, with a sandy texture. At x20 magnification the paste contains a moderate density of fine, rounded, well-sorted quartz sand intermixed with sparse rounded iron grains.

SAND3: A moderately hard, brownish-orange ware with a darker brown exterior surface. The paste contains a sparse frequency of ill-sorted, rounded, quartz up to 1mm in size, very rare limestone and sparse to moderate dark brown, rounded ferruginous pellets.

SAND4: A moderately hard, black sandy ware with a dark reddish-brown core. In the hand the fabric has a slightly sparkling quality. At x20 the paste contains a common frequency of fine, rounded to sub-angular, polished quartz sand, some grains with slight iron-staining.

Early-Middle Bronze Age

The earliest sherd identified is a small bodysherd with comb-impressed decoration from an Early Bronze Age Beaker (Fig. 15.1). The sherd occurs redeposited in a Roman context (2269). The fabric is grog-tempered (GROG1).

The presence of thick-walled base sherds from single vessels in at least two locations (2223 and 2786) suggests the presence of *in situ* urn material, probably of Middle Bronze Age origin. Fill 2223 of the pit for Burial 5 produced 75 sherds (660g) from the base of a cremation urn (Fig. 15.2). A sherd, probably from the same vessel, was found redeposited in posthole 2148 of Structure 1. The fabric is particularly unusual in that the paste contains large fragments of dolerite (ROCK), a rock type foreign to this area, suggesting the vessel, or its constituents, had been imported (see the petrological report above). The radiocarbon dates from associated Burial 1, which indicate a date of 1388–1128 cal. BC, confirm a likely Middle Bronze Age date.

Fill 2786 of pit 2785 contained 23 sherds (164g), again mainly from the base of a large vessel, although in this instance in an oxidised grog and limestone-tempered fabric (GRCALC). The presence of a slightly angled wallsherd (Fig. 15.3) in the same deposit suggests a biconical urn.

Other featured sherds which may belong to the same phase include a single flint and grog-tempered thick-walled sherd decorated with an applied pinched cordon (Fig. 15.4) from ditch 2140. This was the only flint-tempered sherd present on the site and again may be from an imported vessel. It was associated with small fragments of grog and limestone-tempered ware, grog-tempered ware and micaceous sandy ware although the latter is too small to be sure it is pottery.

Amongst the unfeatured sherds most of the grog-tempered sherds, which are not early Roman, are likely to belong to this phase of activity. Posthole 3056 contained a single grog-tempered sherd and could potentially date to the Middle Bronze Age. Most of the other sherds are redeposited in later contexts.

Thick-walled bodysherds with a calcareous paste including Jurassic limestone and fossil shell (CALC1) may also belong to this phase of occupation. The only featured sherds are a base sherd with dimensions similar to those of the urn material (Fig. 15.5) and a small rim fragment (Fig. 15.6). Conversely these could belong to the later Bronze Age period.

Late Bronze Age/Early-Middle Iron Age
The remaining prehistoric sherds are likely to belong to the Late Bronze Age or Early to Middle Iron Age. Apart from a probably residual single Middle Iron Age rim from posthole 2905 there is no featured material. The fabrics divide into calcareous types and sandy wares. The calcareous wares dominate and include limestone and shell, and oolitic-limestone types. The fabrics tend to be more compact and the vessels thinner walled compared to the Middle Bronze Age material. A small quantity of Malvernian rock-tempered ware is present which could be of Middle Iron Age date or later and some Malvernian limestone-tempered ware, which could be of later Iron Age or Early Roman currency.

The small quantity of pottery identified as belonging to the Late Bronze Age to Early Iron Age was associated with the postholes of Structures 1, 4 and 5 (Period 3). Structure 1 produced 26 sherds (98g), of which at least one dates to the Middle Bronze Age (see above). Of the remainder, seventeen are in calcareous fabrics and eight in sandy fabrics. Structure 3, which may be part of the same complex, and Structure 2 produced no ceramic material. Structure 4 produced ten sherds (30g), nine calcareous and one sandy, whilst Structure 5 produced nine sherds (28g), of which six were calcareous and three sandy.

Other miscellaneous features with potentially contemporary assemblages include the two sinuous gullies (2393 and 2395). Gully 2393 produced a tiny scrap of sandy ware (1g) but gully 2395 produced six sherds, again extremely small, each sherd 1g or less, but probably including calcareous and sandy fabrics. Other isolated features yielding sherds solely of later prehistoric character include postholes 2836 (n.i.), 2081 (n.i.), 2245, 2339 (n.i.), 2905 (n.i.), 3189 (n.i.), pit 2420, curvilinear gully 3199, ditch 3293 (n.i.), and tree-hole 2045 (n.i.). (Those features followed by (n.i.) are not illustrated on the plans.)

The only rim (Fig. 15.7) in an oolitic-limestone fabric appears typologically to be a Middle Iron Age form. A small number of features produced just reduced Malvernian sherds, in particular posthole 3255 and ditches 2899 and 3248, which could potentially date back to the Middle Iron Age. By the same token some of the limestone-tempered wares discussed above could continue into the Middle Iron Age.

Discussion

The isolated sherd of Beaker is not particularly significant as a background scatter of such sherds frequently occurs on later sites in the area. Comparable material of Middle Bronze Age date is sparse from the immediate locality. A small group of sherds, radiocarbon-dated to the Middle Bronze Age, has recently been published from a site near Birdlip on the Cotswold scarp (Woodward 1998, 66–7). The sherds are from at least two urn-type vessels belonging to the collared or biconical traditions. The fabrics have sparse grog-tempering. Other biconical urns from Gloucestershire such as those from Swell barrow 1 or Bevan's Quarry, Temple Guiting (O'Neil 1967) have fossil shell-tempered fabrics. The latter assemblage includes vessels with finger-tip impressed applied shoulder cordons. The Bevan's Quarry group is considered by Ellison (1984, 122) to have affinity with the Thames Valley assemblages. In the Thames Valley the biconical urn, which appears in the Early Bronze Age, continues to occur alongside the bucket urns of the Middle Bronze Age. Woodward (1998, 66) thinks it likely that a similar process occurs in Gloucestershire.

Possible Middle Bronze Age occupation has been identified below the Roman villa at Hucclecote (Clifford 1933, 331–2). Although not described in full the pottery appears to include cordoned urn-type material (ibid., Fig. 23). Further afield Middle Bronze Age occupation has been found at Sandy Lane, Charlton Kings (Leah and Young 2001).

The later prehistoric assemblage from the Link Road is really too small and scrappy to draw many conclusions from. At most there are some 70 to 80 sherds. The radiocarbon dates from Structure 1 or Structure 3 confirm activity of Late Bronze Age/Early Iron Age date and this pottery, particularly that from Structure 1, has been used as a yardstick with which to add other sherds.

Other contemporary sites from the region such as the burnt mound at Sandy Lane, Charlton Kings (Timby 2001) and Shorncote, near Cirencester (Morris 1994) have similarly been characterised by a diversity of fabrics. At Sandy Lane, Jurassic shell and limestone, Malvernian rock, grog, grog and shell, sandstone and quartz sand, as well as fine sandy untempered wares were recorded. Shorncote shows a similar range with, in addition, calcite and flint but no sandstone or Malvernian fabrics. Both at Shorncote and Crickley Hill (Elsdon 1994, 207), the local Jurassic limestone fabric dominates although sandy wares are present. Sandy wares, however, are much more frequent from the Late Bronze Age/Early Iron Age site at Lechlade (Hingley 1986; Timby 1998a) where there is a marked fine sandy fine ware component to the assemblage but perhaps less overall diversity of fabric. There are clearly differences between apparently contemporary sites but unfortunately the character of the present group is not able to add much to the overall developing picture.

The presence of a small quantity of Malvernian ware, both rock-tempered and limestone-tempered might intimate a Middle Iron Age presence, but conversely may belong with the Late Iron Age/Early Roman phase of occupation.

Catalogue of illustrated prehistoric sherds (Fig. 15)

1. Small Beaker bodysherd with comb-impressed decoration. Black interior and inner core, dark red-brown exterior. Fabric: GROG1. Redeposited in fill 2269 of Romano-British Burial 3 (2267), Period 4.3.
2. Basesherd from a large vessel, probably an urn. Fabric: ROCK. Cremation Burial 5, fill 2223 of pit 2222, Period 2.
3. Bodysherd from a moderately large, thick-walled vessel showing a slight wall carination. Fabric: GROG2. Orange exterior, dark brown inner surface and core. Fill 2786 of pit 2785, Period 2.
4. Bodysherd decorated with a finger pinched ?cordon. Fabric: FLGR. Fill 2141 of ditch 2140, Period 3.
5. Basesherd from a closed form. Fabric: CALC1. Fill 2158 of posthole 2157, Period 3.
6. Small everted rimsherd. Fabric: CALC1. Oxidised throughout. Fill 1005 of ditch 1004/2199, Period 4.3.
7. Rim probably from a handmade globular bodied jar. Fabric: CALC2. Fill 2906 of posthole 2905, Periods 4.1 to 4.3.

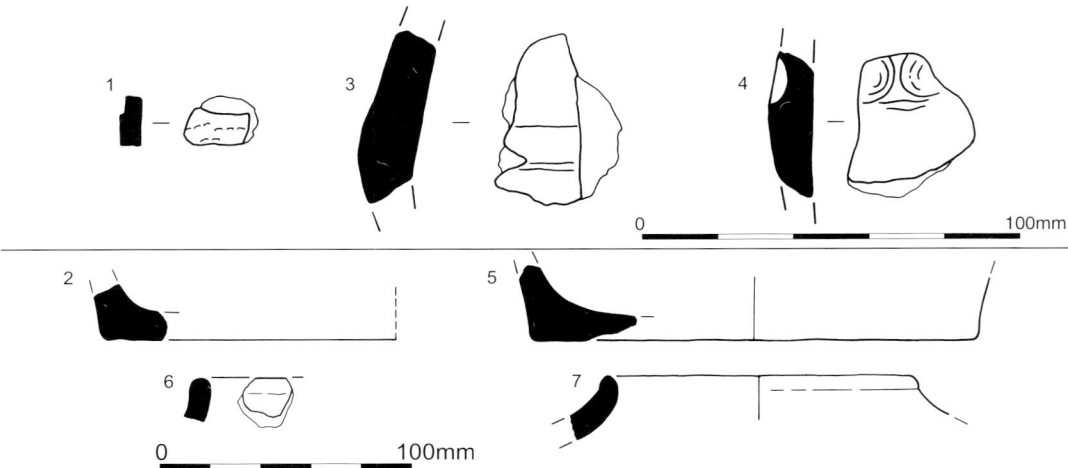

Fig. 15: Prehistoric pottery, nos 1–7 (1, 3 and 4, scale 1:2; 2, 5, 6 and 7, scale 1:3)

Roman

Roman wares account for 95% of the total assemblage with wares spanning the 1st to 4th centuries AD. The assemblage is dominated by locally produced Severn Valley wares, a long-lived and conservative industry whose products are often difficult to date precisely, especially if the material is fragmentary.

Although rural in character, the settlement received a small amount of imported wares. Continental imports include Spanish Dressel 20 olive-oil amphora, Gallic wine amphora, North Gaulish mortaria, and samian. Regional imports include in the early Roman period products from the Wiltshire industries, the Malvern area, Verulamium and Poole Harbour (Dorset Black-Burnished ware). In the later Roman period the site was supplied with vessels from the large regional industries, in particular Oxfordshire, Nene Valley and Dorset Black-Burnished ware. A complete absence of later 4th-century shelly ware and only a limited range of forms in the Oxfordshire wares suggests that intensive occupation had ceased well before *c.* AD 360, perhaps even in the first two decades of the 4th century, although a few 4th-century coins testify to spasmodic activity into the latter part of that century.

Table 3: Quantified summary of fabrics.

*Weight (Wt) is in grammes. EVE = Rim estimated vessel equivalent. The fabric codes follow the nomenclature of Tomber and Dore (1998). A concordance is provided with the Gloucester type fabric series (Glos TF). * = less than 1%*

Type	Fabric	Description	Glos TF	No	%	Wt	%	EVE	%
PREHISTORIC		see Table 2							
Sub-total				256		1676		10	
ROMAN									
Native (handmade)	GROG	grog-tempered	2A-C	51	*	202	*	17	*
	MAL L1	Malvernian limestone	33	164	3	482	1	23	*
	MAL L2	Malvernian limestone	216	3	*	32	*	0	*
	MAL REA	Malvernian rock-tempered	18	12	*	76	*	14	*
Local	GLOS OX	Gloucester oxidised ware	11A	20	*	135	*	10	*
	GLOS MIL	Kingsholm military ware	24	2	8	50	*	25	*
	SVW OX	Severn Valley ware (oxidised)	11B	2908	55	30542	62	1627	43
	SVW EA	Severn Valley ware early variant	11D	106	2	550	1	68	2
	SVW RE	Severn Valley ware (reduced)	11B	483	9	3310	7	572	15
	OXID	local oxidised wares	-	12	*	65	*	0	0
	GREY	local grey sandy wares	-	118	2	920	2	27	*
	MICGW	micaceous greyware	5	280	5	2481	5	309	8
Regional	SAV GT	Savernake ware	6	19	*	563	1	20	*
	MALV RO	Malvernian wheelmade	19	28	8	504	1	50	1
	DOR BB1	Dorset Black-Burnished	4	833	16	6078	12	751	20
	LNV CC	Lower Nene Valley colour coat	12B	1	*	5	*	0	0
	OXF PA	Oxfordshire parchment ware	1A	4	*	31	*	0	0
	OXF RC	Oxfordshire colour-coated ware	12A	53	1	411	*	42	1
	OXF WH	Oxfordshire whiteware	13/9A	22	*	349	*	28	*
	SW OXWS	South-west white-slipped, oxidised	15a	4	*	14	*	0	0
	WIL OX	North Wiltshire oxidised	232	21	*	57	*	12	*
	WIL RE	North Wiltshire reduced	231	38	*	261	*	40	1
	WIL BB1	Wiltshire Black-Burnished ware	201	17	*	76	*	0	0
	VER WH	Verulamium whiteware	9F	2	*	260	*	15	*
Import	BAT AM	Dressel 20 amphora	10A	15	*	1170	2	0	0
	GAL AM	Gallic amphora	10B	2	*	128	*	0	0
	AM MISC	miscellaneous amphora	10	1	*	7	*	0	0
	NOG WH	North Gaulish mortaria	9C	2	*	22	*	0	0
	SAM	Gaulish samian	8	71	1	583	1	69	2
Source unknown	CC	miscellaneous colour-coated ware	12	1	*	3	*	0	0
	WSLIP	white-slipped oxidised ware	-	2	*	6	*	3	*
	WW	whiteware	-	2	*	14	*	27	*
	MISC	other miscellaneous	-	13	*	51	*	0	0
Sub-total				5310	100	49438	100	3749	100
MEDIEVAL	MED	medieval		10		48		0	
POST-MED	PMED	post-medieval		2		3		0	
Sub-total				12		51		0	
Total				5578		51165		3759	

Roman fabrics

A summary of all the fabrics recorded can be found in Table 3. No further descriptions are given for the well-known named traded wares for which further details can be found in Tomber and Dore (1998).

IMPORTED WARES
Samian. Mainly plain Central Gaulish wares but with one or two South Gaulish pieces. Very abraded.
Dressel 20 amphora (BAT AM; Tomber and Dore 1998, 84–6).
Gallic amphora (GAL AM; Tomber and Dore 1998, 93–5).
North Gaulish whiteware (NOG WH; Tomber and Dore 1998, 75–6).

REGIONAL WARES
Malvernian rock-tempered ware (MAL REA; Peacock 1967, type A; Tomber and Dore 1998, 147).
Malvernian limestone-tempered ware (MAL L1; MAL L2; Peacock 1967, type B; Spencer 1983).
Malvernian wheelmade Roman wares (MAL RO).
Dorset Black-Burnished ware (DOR BB1; Tomber and Dore 1998, 127).
Savernake ware (SAV GT; Tomber and Dore 1998, 191).
Wiltshire grey sandy ware (WIL RE).
Wiltshire oxidised sandy ware (WIL OX).
Wiltshire wheelmade Black-Burnished ware (WIL BB1).
South-west white-slipped ware (SOW WS; Tomber and Dore 1998, 192).
Oxfordshire whiteware (OXF WH; Tomber and Dore 1998, 174; Young 1977).
Oxfordshire colour-coated ware (Tomber and Dore 1998, 174; Young 1977).
Oxfordshire parchment ware (Tomber and Dore 1998, 174; Young 1977).
Lower Nene Valley colour-coated ware (LNV CC; Tomber and Dore 1998, 118).
Verulamium whiteware (VER WH; Tomber and Dore 1998, 154).
Miscellaneous whiteware (WHITE).

LOCAL WARES
Grog-tempered handmade native ware (GROG).
Severn Valley wares (oxidised) (SVW OX; Tomber and Dore 1998, 149).
Severn Valley ware (reduced) (SVW RE).
Early variants of Severn Valley ware (SVW EA).
Micaceous greyware (MIC GW).
Gloucester City oxidised ware (GLOS OX; Gloucester type fabric 11A; Timby 1991).
Kingsholm military ware (GLOS MIL; Gloucester type fabric 24; Darling 1985, 78).

Discussion by period

PERIOD 4.1: 1ST CENTURY AD
The earliest Roman assemblage belongs to the 1st century AD. The high proportion of native ware, both limestone and grog-tempered, along with early Severn Valley wares might suggest a pre-conquest phase of use which would be indistinguishable ceramically. In rural sites many of the Late Iron Age traditions continue up to the 2nd century AD. The pottery from Period 4.1 (Table 4) shows very little diversity in fabric. Severn Valley wares account for 61% by sherd count (82% by weight). Handmade Malvernian wares are moderately well represented accounting for 20.5% by count (5% by weight) while grog-tempered wares account for a further 6%.

The features can perhaps, on the basis of the pottery, be split into those which include Roman wares proper in their assemblages and those which appear more indigenous. Features which fall into the latter category include pits 3273, 2613 and gullies 2899 and 2640. Features

Table 4: Occurrence of Roman wares by period
  Weight (Wt) is in grammes. EVE = Rim estimated vessel equivalent. Fabric codes after Tomber and Dore (1998)

Type	Fabric	4.1			4.2			4.3			4.1-4.3			5		
		No.	Wt	EVE	No.	Wt	EVE	No.	Wt	EVE	No.	Wt	EVE	No.	Wt	EVE
ROMAN																
Import	SAM	0	0	0	4	99	18	58	426	48	5	30	0	2	18	0
	BAT AM	0	0	0	1	412	0	13	746	0	1	12	0	0	0	0
	GAL AM	0	0	0	0	0	0	1	125	0	0	0	0	1	3	0
	NOG WH	0	0	0	0	0	0	2	22	0	0	0	0	0	0	0
Regional	MAL LI	35	73	4	11	18	0	114	444	19	12	27	0	4	5	0
	MAL RE A	2	9	2	0	0	0	5	37	12	2	10	0	0	0	0
	MAL RO	0	0	0	0	0	0	19	212	42	7	62	8	1	218	0
	DOR BB1	2	7	0	93	1005	151	652	4496	528	62	464	67	15	61	0
	SAV GT	0	0	0	0	0	0	16	510	15	2	36	5	0	0	0
	WIL RE	1	3	0	6	78	25	29	161	15	0	0	0	1	3	0
	WIL OX	6	12	0	0	0	0	14	43	0	1	2	12	0	0	0
	WIL BB1	0	0	0	0	0	0	14	69	0	1	3	0	2	4	0
	SOW WS	0	0	0	0	0	0	4	14	0	0	0	0	0	0	0
	OXF WH	0	0	0	0	0	0	11	78	0	0	0	0	1	2	0
	OXF WHM	0	0	0	1	70	20	9	199	8	0	0	0	0	0	0
	OXF RC	0	0	0	0	0	0	41	317	42	1	1	0	1	2	0
	OXF PA	0	0	0	0	0	0	4	31	0	0	0	0	0	0	0
	LNV CC	0	0	0	0	0	0	1	5	0	0	0	0	0	0	0
	VER WH	0	0	0	0	0	0	2	260	15	0	0	0	0	0	0
	WHITE	1	13	27	0	0	0	1	1	0	0	0	0	0	0	0
Local	GROG	11	50	7	20	107	3	33	166	7	2	10	0	4	11	0
	SVW EA	6	15	10	3	23	6	69	367	0	25	136	40	2	9	0
	SVW OX	98	1158	114	242	3187	122	2241	23146	1136	161	1557	177	143	1302	65
	SVW RE	6	150	0	99	1001	142	349	1922	414	9	61	0	15	76	0
	MICGW	0	0	0	3	18	0	245	2296	302	31	250	23	3	10	0
	GLOS OX	4	28	0	1	6	5	13	94	0	2	7	5	0	0	0
	GLOS MIL	1	35	25	0	0	0	1	15	0	0	0	0	0	0	0
Source Unknown	unidentif	0	0	0	3	7	0	2	41	0	0	0	0	3	4	0
	GREY	1	6	0	15	200	0	89	632	19	10	69	5	2	6	0
	OXID	0	0	0	1	23	0	7	36	0	0	0	0	0	0	0
	CC	0	0	0	0	0	0	0	0	0	1	3	0	0	0	0
	WSLIP	0	0	0	0	0	0	1	3	0	0	0	0	0	0	0
MED/PMED	various	0	0	0	0	0	0	3	27	0	1	2	0	8	22	0
Total		174	1559	189	503	6254	492	4063	36941	2622	336	2742	342	208	1756	65

with Roman wares proper include gullies 2409 and 3248, ditch 2921, and pits 3225, 3287 and 3374.

Gully 2409 of ?RH1 produced a small assemblage of 26 sherds among which were Malvernian wares, Dorset Black-Burnished ware (DOR BB1) and the only imported whiteware butt beaker (Camulodunum type 113) on the site (Fig. 16.8). This may be a product of the Verulamium kilns. In addition there was a sherd of grey, fine, sandy ware, possibly North Wiltshire or early Oxfordshire, decorated with a barbotine circle. A date in the later 1st or early 2nd century AD is likely for the abandonment of this feature, if it is accepted that DOR BB1 is in circulation at this time.

Of particular interest is the presence of Gloucester kiln-type oxidised ware (Gloucester type fabric 11A) (Timby 1991) from pits 3374 and 3225 and a sherd from a Hofheim type flagon in Kingsholm military-type ware (Gloucester type fabric 24) also from pit 3374 (Fig. 16.9). The fabric and form of the latter suggest a Claudio-Neronian date. Gloucester kiln wares were produced from the immediate pre-Flavian period but continued to be made into the 2nd century. These wares have rarely been identified from sites outside Gloucester City. Other vessels from pit 3374 include handmade and wheelmade storage jars in SVW OX (Fig. 16.10–12), a necked cordoned jar and a tankard also in SVW OX.

PERIOD 4.2: EARLY 2ND CENTURY AD

An assemblage of 503 sherds (6254g) was recovered from Period 4.2 features. The average sherd size is greater than that of Period 4.1 at 12.4g compared with 9g indicating slightly better preservation, although it is still not good. Samian appears for the first time, albeit very small fragments, and there is a single large sherd from a Dressel 20 olive-oil amphora. While most of the samian appears to be of Central Gaulish manufacture there are occasional fragments of South Gaulish wares. The assemblage also shows an increased number of Dorset Black-Burnished wares and products from Wiltshire. Severn Valley ware continues to dominate accounting for 50% (count) of the group, while DOR BB1 accounts for a further 18%. Native wares including Malvernian limestone and grog-tempered wares are still well represented.

An assemblage of 163 sherds, recovered from gully 2369, includes oxidised and reduced Severn Valley ware featuring dishes, several tankards, everted-rimmed jars, beakers, lids and flanged and flat-rimmed bowls (Fig. 16.14–16). In total Severn Valley ware accounts for 78.5% of the assemblage from this ditch. The only other wares present are DOR BB1, samian, a Wiltshire greyware dish, and an oxidised basesherd in an orange sandy ware carrying part of a potter's stamp (illegible).

PERIOD 4.3: 2ND TO EARLY 4TH CENTURY AD

Period 4.3 produced the largest overall quantity of material with 4063 sherds, 37kg in weight. The pottery shows a greater diversity with an increase in traded wares. There is a relatively high residual component, reflected in the low average sherd size of just 9g. Amongst the continental traded wares are samian, Dressel 20 and Gaulish wine amphorae, and a North Gaulish mortarium. Regional imports include two Verulamium mortarium sherds, one stamped (Fig. 16.30), and a single sherd of Nene Valley colour-coated ware. Dorset Black-Burnished ware remains at levels not dissimilar to Period 4.2 accounting for 16% count (12% weight). It includes mainly jar forms with acute lattice or diagonal burnished line decoration (Fig. 16.32), plain-rimmed dishes, lids (Fig. 16.27–8), flat-rimmed bowls and conical flanged bowls. The forms range in date from the later 2nd through to the early 4th century. One jar has an internally sooted base.

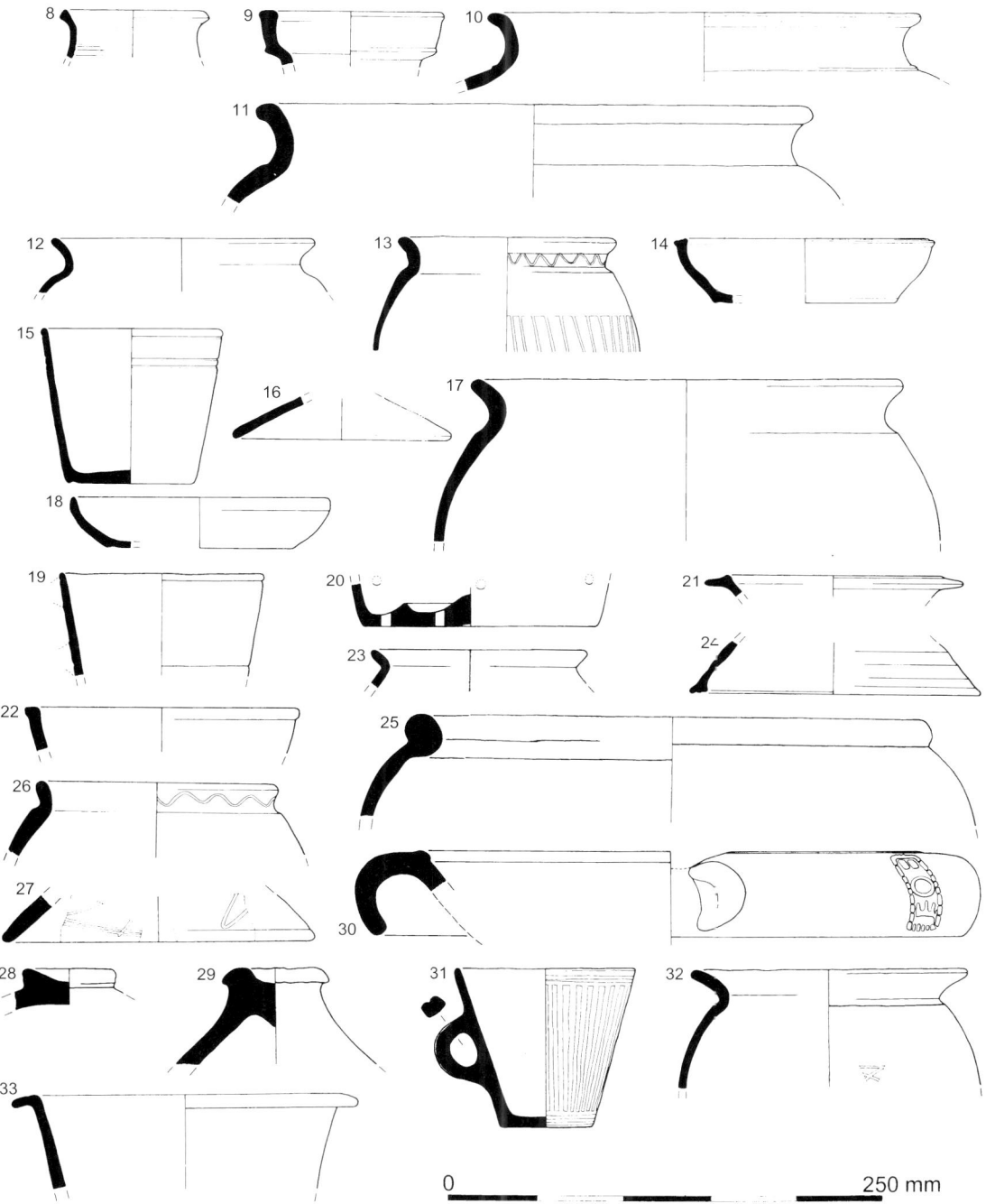

Fig. 16: Roman pottery, nos 8–33 (scale 1:4)

Severn Valley wares are still very common, making up 65% by count (or 68.5% by weight) of the group. A variety of forms are present including curved-walled dishes (Fig. 17.34), tankards (Fig. 16.31), beakers, bowls, everted-rimmed and triangular-rimmed jars. Amongst the other local wares are handmade and wheelmade Malvernian wares both as jars and lids (Fig. 16.29) and several grey micaceous wares (Fig. 16.33, 17.35) typical of assemblages dating from the later 2nd to 4th century AD in this area.

The presence of Oxfordshire colour-coated wares (OXF RC) and parchment wares (OXF PA) suggests that certain features were not abandoned until at least the early 4th century. Features containing these late sherds include ditches 3044 (n.i.) and 3047 (n.i.) within Enclosure C, gully 2280 in Enclosure D, ditch 2365 and pit 2465. The Oxfordshire colour coats are restricted to Young (1977) bowl forms C45 and C51.

The largest single assemblage came from the midden which produced 776 sherds (8kg) (Fig. 16.17–26). It contained a variety of wares again dominated by oxidised Severn Valley ware (82% by weight). The oxidised Severn Valley ware forms were surprisingly diverse with storage jar, narrow-mouthed everted rimmed jars, tankards, jugs, beakers, hemispherical flanged bowls, reeded-rimmed bowls, shallow dishes and a cheese-press represented. Quite a high proportion (17 sherds, 212g) of samian was present, with Dragendorff forms 18, 31, 37 and 27. Dressel 20 amphora sherds and the single North Gaulish mortaria also came from this group along with an Oxfordshire whiteware mortaria (Young 1977, form M22). This is perhaps one of the latest vessels in the group with a date range *c*. AD 240–400. The midden seems to have largely accumulated during the first half of the 3rd century.

Catalogue of illustrated Roman sherds (Figs 16–17)

8. Whiteware butt beaker, Camulodunum type 113, possibly a Verulamium whiteware. Fill 2615 of gully 2409, Period 4.1.
9. Collared rim flagon in a fabric similar to Glos TF 24, [GLOSMIL]. Fill 3375 of pit 3374, Period 4.1.
10. Handmade, necked cordoned jar, SVW OX. Fill 3375 of pit 3374, Period 4.1.
11. Handmade everted rim storage jar, SVW OX. Fill 3375 of pit 3374, Period 4.1.
12. Wheelmade everted rim, wide-mouthed jar, SVW OX. Fill 3375 of pit 3374, Period 4.1.
13. Jar, DOR BB1 decorated with diagonal burnished lines. Fill 2543 of ditch 2542, Period 4.2.
14. Dish with a narrow, reeded rim. SVO OX. Fill 2389 of ditch 2369, Period 4.2.
15. Grey Severn Valley ware tankard. SVW RE. Fill 2397 of ditch 2369, Period 4.2.
16. Blackened lid with some spalling. Severn Valley ware variant. SVW RE. Fill 2397 of ditch 2369, Period 4.2.

Nos 17-26 are all from the midden (fill 2849 of feature 2848), Period 4.3.
17. Handmade storage jar, SVW OX.
18. Curved wall dish, SVW OX.
19. Handled tankard, SVW OX.
20. Cheese press, SVW OX.
21. Flanged bowl, SVW RE.
22. Dish, SVW OX.
23. Everted rimmed grey beaker, SVW RE.
24. Greyware lid, SVW RE.
25. Beaded-rimmed wheelmade jar, SAV GT.
26. Jar, DOR BB1.
27. Lid, DOR BB1. Fill 2500 of ditch 2371, Period 4.3.
28. Lid, DOR BB1. Fill 2540 of ditch 2371, Period 4.3.
29. Knob from a large, handmade, conical lid, MALV RO. Fill 2472 of recut of ditch 2365, Period 4.3.

30. Flange from a whiteware mortaria (VER WH) with a worn potter's stamp close to the spout area. Retrograde FECITE ? Fill 3335 of ditch 2365, Period 4.3. SF 103.
31. Black micaceous handled tankard, vertically burnished. SVW RE. Fill 2406 of ditch 2405, Period 4.3.
32. Jar, DOR BB1. Fill 2406 of ditch 2405, Period 4.3.
33. Grooved-rimmed bowl unevenly coloured with a black interior and orange-brown exterior with black patches. MIC GW. Fill 2406 of ditch 2405, Period 4.3.
34. Grooved-rimmed dish, SVW OX. Fill 2406 of ditch 2405, Period 4.3.
35. Grey, flanged, sandy, micaceous bowl. Fill 2480 of gully 2474, Period 4.3.

Fired clay object (Fig. 17)

36. Perforated disk made from a sherd of Severn Valley ware (SVW OX). Fill 2285 of ditch 2284, Period 4.3.

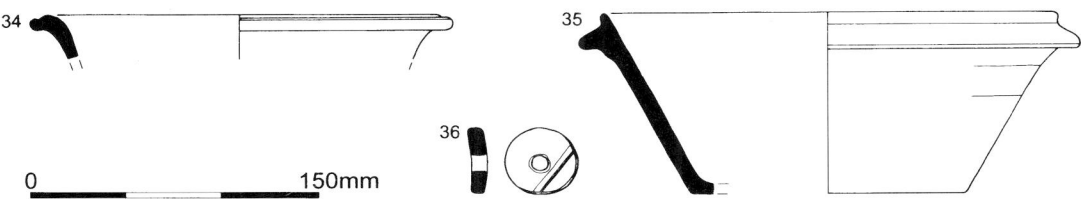

Fig. 17: Roman pottery nos 34–35 and fired clay object 36 (scale 1:4)

Regional discussion

The Roman assemblage from the Link Road is an important addition to the area. Excavation has revealed an increasing number of sites in the hinterland of Gloucester that were occupied in the 1st century AD and produce a combination of native wares and early Severn Valley wares, for example Saintbridge, Abbeydale III and Coppice Corner (Kingsholm). In addition several Roman sites in the locality have been investigated, in particular Barnwood (Clifford 1930), Well's Bridge (Rawes 1977), Hucclecote (Clifford 1933), and Brockworth (Rawes 1981). While some notion of the range of wares present can be gleaned from the published reports, none of the assemblages has been subjected to modern analysis and quantified information is lacking. Slightly further afield recent work has taken place on the top of the Cotswold scarp at Cowley (Mudd *et al.* 1999) and on material from older excavations at Great Witcombe villa (Leach 1998).

At the latter two sites, and probably all the sites mentioned, Severn Valley wares (SVW OX) in particular, and Dorset Black-Burnished ware (DOR BB1) to a lesser extent, dominate the assemblages. At the current site these account for 70% and 12% of the Roman assemblage by weight respectively (see Table 3). At Cowley SVW OX accounted for 30% by weight and DOR BB1 for 29% (Timby 1999a). At Great Witcombe, which is largely a late Roman assemblage, SVW OX varied between 42% and 50% and DOR BB1 between 20% and 34% per period (Leach 1998, 66). Both these sites were occupied up to the last quarter of the 4th century, unlike the Link Road site, and consequently later products like the Oxfordshire colour-coated wares are better represented. What does appear to be emerging from these figures is that there is a marked decrease in the amount of Severn Valley ware reaching sites on the top of the scarp. This is further reflected in material from Cirencester where Severn Valley ware is quite rare and at Kingscote, located up on the Cotswolds to the south-west, where SVW OX only accounts for 10% of the assemblage (Timby 1998b). Other sites on the Severn Plain such as Frocester and Gloucester City appear to be well served by the SVW OX industries. By contrast DOR BB1 seems to increase towards Cirencester where later Roman assemblages have between 25% and 45% (by estimated vessel equivalent) (Cooper 1998). This observation supports the suggestion that the Fosse Way featured prominently in the distribution of DOR BB1 (Allen and Fulford 1996).

The number of Wiltshire wares at the site is perhaps a little surprising and does suggest links to the east over the Cotswold scarp. Gloucester City has produced very few Wiltshire products whereas they dominate the Cirencester assemblages.

The nearby site at Brockworth (Rawes 1981) probably shows a very similar pottery profile to the Link Road although the former appears to have been occupied into the later 4th to 5th century. Possible Gloucester products may also be present at Brockworth, for example a ring-necked flagon (Rawes 1981, Fig. 6.11) and mica-dusted ware (ibid., Fig. 7.30–1). Samian is also well in evidence and the site was supplied with Dressel 20 amphora.

It would seem that while these hinterland sites do not show quite the richness and diversity of wares found at the major urban centres such as Gloucester and Cirencester, they were relatively well furnished in terms of having a small quantity of imported material. The villas, such as Great Witcombe, appear to have a slightly more diverse range of imports compared to the assemblages from sites such as the Link Road and Brockworth, perhaps suggesting that the perceived quality of the pottery assemblages may have some relationship to site status.

The Coins, by Peter Guest

Six copper-alloy coins of Roman date were recovered. Details are listed in Table 5.

Table 5: The coins
References: Cu. = Besly and Bland 1983; CHK = Carson et al. 1960; RIC = Bruun 1966

Context	Denomination	Date	Obverse	Reverse	Mint mark	Mint	Reference
2852	sestertius	117-38	Hadrian	illegible	-	-	-
2439	radiate	260-8	Postumus	Saeculi Felicitas	-	-	Cu. 2444
3329	radiate	273-4	Tetricus II	Pietas Augg	-	-	-
unstrat	AE2	313-4	Constantine I	SOLI INVICTO COMITI	S / F / PLN	London	RIC: 10
furrow	AE3 copy	(330-40)	as Urbs Roma	as wolf & twins	// TR.S	as Trier	as CHK: 65
3321	AE3	367-75	Gratian	GLORIA NOVI SAECVLI	[.....]	Arles	-

The Metalwork, by Nina Crummy

The assemblage is divided into three groups: grave goods deposited with the inhumations, coffin nails, and objects from the other features on the site. The catalogue entries for the grave goods and coffin nails are contained in the grave catalogue above.

Grave goods

Two burials contained hobnails from footwear. It is not possible to determine what type of shoes might have been deposited as the soles of both closed shoes and sandals were nailed. However, the high number (103) of nails and nail fragments from Burial 3 suggests that they were from soles set with a row of hobnails around the margin and perhaps with a pattern of nails within this frame (MacConnoran 1986, 218), while the 25 nails from Burial 16 might be from similar, though less heavily nailed soles (Rhodes 1980, 559, Fig. 60).

Burial 16 also contained a trumpet brooch of late 1st or early 2nd-century date (Fig. 13.1). It is closely similar to two examples from Hampshire, both with the same slender cruciform foot, rectangular plate below the head-loop, and clearly-defined frontal button. One is from Silchester and appears to be a direct parallel to the Gloucester brooch (Hull forthcoming, 4861), while the other, from Winchester, has one more moulding to the foot-knob and is slightly larger (Hattatt 1987, 135, Fig. 44.960).

Burial 9 contained a penannular armlet with snake's head terminals and a short fragment of an iron strip. The full size and function of the latter are unknown. The armlet (Fig. 11.1) is a very plain form of Johns' type Bii, which developed in the 2nd century and continued in use until the late 3rd or early 4th century (Johns 1996, 109–11). It may have been credited with specifically apotropaic powers, as the snake is an emblem of the after-life and rebirth, and is also associated with healing. A pair of snakes appear on the caduceus carried by both Mercury and Aesculapius, and the healing goddess Salus is often shown feeding a snake (Toynbee 1973, 234).

From Burial 15 came a group of decayed and fragmentary iron fittings from a fairly substantial, if simply made, wooden box (Fig. 12.1–7). The fitting to retain the bolt is very large, and one clenched nail shaft suggests that the boards used were at least 25mm thick. This is comparable to the board thickness of a late Roman box from Colchester (Crummy 1983, 87–8). Interlinked double-spiked loops were used for the hinges, and the lid was fitted with an iron drop-handle. Fragments of iron sheet may be from a lock-plate or corner-plates. No trace of contents was found.

While this box does not appear to have been used to contain cremated ashes, the closest parallels for many of these fittings are the Antonine cremation caskets from Skeleton Green, Hertfordshire. There, Burial XXX contained an iron drop-handle and simple loop-hinges made with one strap and a split-spike loop, and a cramp was among the fittings in Burial XXXV. Sheet iron plates were used both externally and internally (Borrill 1981, 304–18).

While the use of the inhumation rite for these burials might suggest a date either in the mid 1st century AD or from the 3rd century into the early 5th, the grave goods indicate that Burials 9, 15 and 16 are earlier, probably within a range from the Trajanic to Antonine periods. The rite of depositing a pair of shoes with a corpse is long-lived, so Burial 3 cannot be closely dated other than on stratigraphic grounds.

Coffin nails

Burials 3, 7, 9, 12, 13 and 14 contained iron nails from timber coffins. The two fragments from Burial 16 may either be residual or part of the wooden box. All the surviving nail heads are of Manning's Type 1b, with roughly shaped round/rectangular slightly domed heads (1985, Fig. 32). Few were complete. A list of these nails and others from the site is in the archive.

Also recovered from Burial 14 was part of an iron strap fitted with a nail (Fig. 12.1). Some coffins at Lankhills, Winchester and Poundbury were made with angle-brackets (Clarke 1979, 337; Mills 1993, Figs 83–9), and it is possible that this is a fragment of a similar fitting from coffin construction, though the recovery of only one piece suggests that it was residual in the grave fill rather than directly associated with Burial 14.

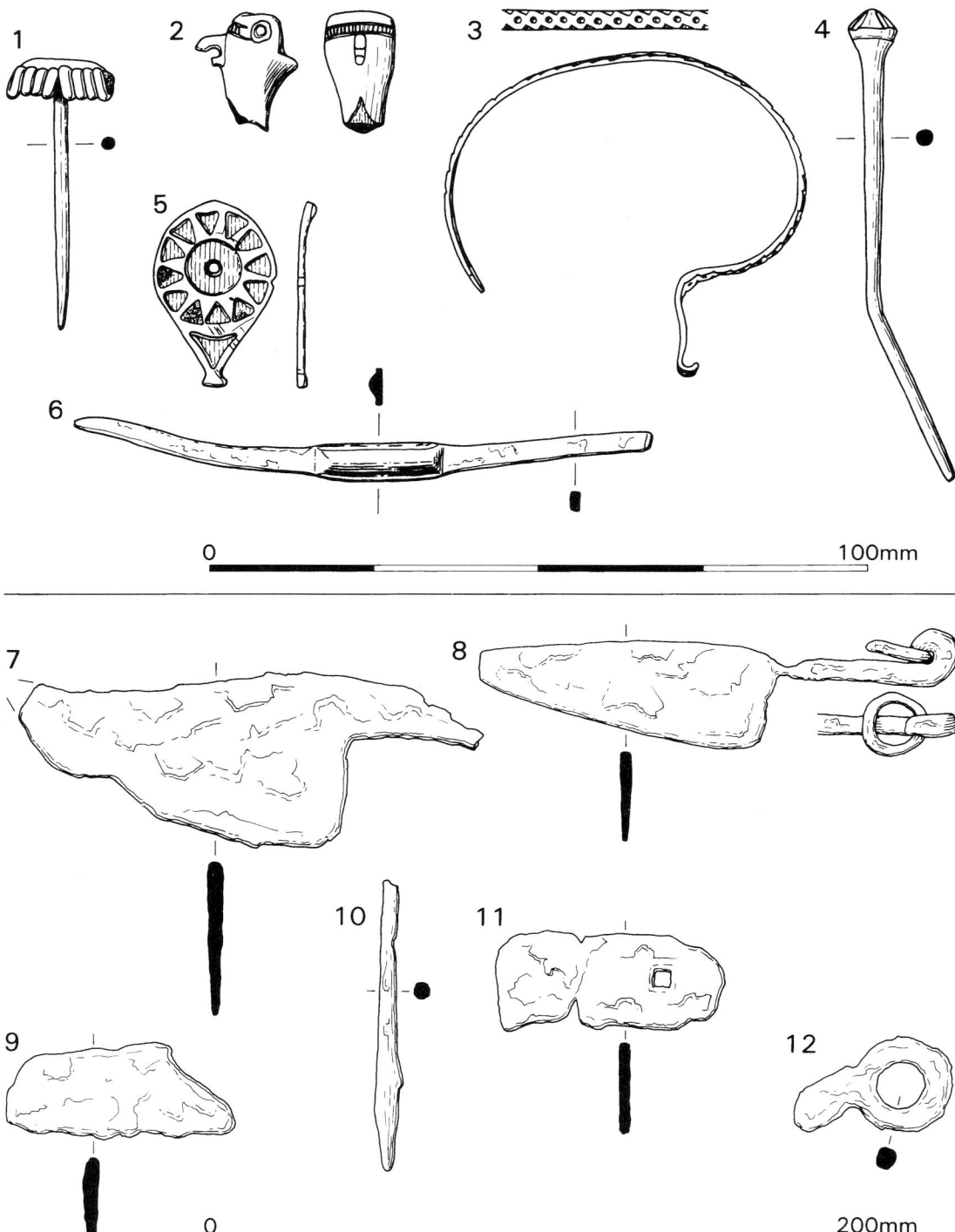

Fig. 18: Objects of copper alloy (scale 1:1) and iron (scale 1:2)

Other finds

The assemblage has a wide date-range, from an iron knife of a form originating in the late Iron Age (Fig. 18.7) and a brooch belonging to the second half of the 1st century (Fig. 18.1) through to a late 4th-century armlet with debased wave-crest decoration (Fig. 18.3) paralleled at Poundbury (Cool and Mills 1993, Fig. 65.8–9), Marshfield (Barford and Hughes 1985, Fig. 47.1), and Colchester (Crummy 1983, Fig. 44.1703–4).

The objects are not very varied in terms of function. Simple personal ornaments are represented by the brooches, armlet and hairpin (Fig. 18.4). The three knives are all quite large, and may have been used in butchery, or for fairly coarse culinary chopping or cutting. Structural fittings are well represented, mainly nails and straps, but also rings, which may be for suspension or attachment. Scraps of sheet lead and some frozen dribbles of molten lead probably indicate nothing more than small-scale plumbing or structural operations in the area. Unalloyed lead was soft and easily worked, but was also strong and easily patched if necessary. It was used for many items associated with water supply, in particular pipes and tanks.

Perhaps surprisingly in such a small assemblage, literacy is demonstrated by two iron stylus fragments (Fig. 18.10 and one not illustrated), and by the 2nd-century piriform seal-box lid (Fig. 18.5). The latter is very similar to an example from Ilchester, where the enamel was preserved and showed alternating red and blue triangles in the outer zone (Leach 1982, Fig. 119.78). A round lid from Great Walsingham, Norfolk, also has the same sunburst decoration with alternating enamel colours (Bagnall Smith 1999, Fig. 5.57).

Catalogue of illustrated metal objects (Fig.18)

1. Copper-alloy spring and pin from a two-piece brooch. The high-set external chord and straight pin suggest this may be from a 1st-century Polden Hill brooch (Hattatt 1987, Fig. 2.16). Length 43mm. Fill 3157 of gully 3153, Period 4.2.
2. Head of a copper-alloy trumpet derivative brooch, with the spring mechanism held between two large side lugs and a small pierced lug at centre front. The head flares out only slightly, and is crossed by a knurled band behind the lug. Length 13mm. Unstratified.
3. Copper-alloy armlet with wave-crest decoration formed by alternating oblique notches on the edges. The inner 'curl' of the wave is shown by a punched or drilled dot. The clasp is of hook-and-eye type, the terminals marked by groups of transverse grooves. Maximum internal diameter (distorted) 53.5mm. Rectangular section, height 3mm, 1mm thick. Fill 2285 of ditch 2365, Period 4.
4. Copper-alloy pin with conical grooved head, Cool's Group 25 (Cool 1990, 170, Fig. 12.11). Tip missing. Length 75mm. This form cannot be closely dated. Fill 2515 of gully 2542, Period 4.2.
5. Piriform copper-alloy seal-box lid with starburst decoration of radiating triangles, obliquely grooved, set around a perforated central circular panel. The metal between these triangles is recessed to take enamel, though only slight traces of the filling remain. The hinge lug has broken off. Length 29.5mm. Fill 3048 of ditch 3047 (Enclosure C), Period 4.3.
6. Copper-alloy strip, slightly curved. The section is rectangular, except at the centre, which is expanded and flanged on either side of a central rounded rib. Length 89mm, maximum width 6mm, 2.5mm thick. Fill 2398 of ditch 2365, Period 4.3.
7. Wide-bladed iron knife with curved tang and concave curve to the back of the blade giving an S-shaped upper profile. The edge curves upwards to the tip, which is missing. There is a slight step on the tang. Length 145mm. This is Manning's Type 24, which originated in the Late Iron Age and continued in use into the early Roman period. There are examples from southern and central Britain, and the type is particularly well represented at Hod Hill (Manning 1985, 118–19). Fill 2849 of midden 2848, Period 4.3.
8. Iron knife with integral handle which ends in a loop, through which passes a suspension ring. The back of the blade is very slightly curved, the wide blade tapers upwards to the tip. Length 161mm. Fill 2285 of ditch 2365, Period 4.3.
9. Iron knife blade fragment, with straight back and edge curving upwards to form the tip. Length 71mm, maximum width 22mm. Fill 2887 of pit 2886, Period 4.2.

10. Iron stylus fragment, with shouldered point. Probably Manning's Type 2 (Manning 1985, Fig. 24). Length 93mm. Fill 2849 of midden 2848, Period 4.3.
11. Two fitting iron strap-hinge fragments, with nail hole at surviving rounded end. Length 69mm, width 28mm. Fill 2281 of gully 2280, Period 4.3.
12. Iron ring with damaged extension. Internal diameter 16mm, 7mm thick. Fill 2386 of ditch 2365, Period 4.3.

Non-illustrated metal objects

Fragment of copper-alloy circular-section ?ring. Length 27.5mm, diameter 4mm. Fill 2484 of ditch 2365, Period 4.3.
Fragment of folded copper-alloy sheet. Maximum dimensions 22 by 21mm. Fill 2386 of ditch 2365, Period 4.3.
Bent and twisted copper-alloy sheet, much damaged, but probably from the top and shoulder of a shouldered vessel with a short neck and everted rim. Maximum dimensions 54mm by 32mm. Fill 2005 of trackway ditch 2199, Period 4.3.
Three pieces of offcut lead sheet, 1mm thick, smooth on both sides: i) more or less rectangular fragment folded neatly in half, maximum dimensions 117 by 46.5mm; ii) as i), but with one edge folded back on itself, maximum dimensions 107 by 47mm; iii) much folded fragment, with five layers in places, maximum dimensions 8 by 41mm. Total weight 167gm. Fill 2849 of midden 2848, Period 4.3.
Two fragments of offcut lead sheet, smooth on both sides: i) roughly triangular, maximum dimensions 62 by 50mm; ii) folded and crumpled, maximum dimensions 65 by 51mm. Total weight 53gm. Fill 2849 of midden 2848, Period 4.3.
Roughly triangular lead dribble, with ridged underside from flowing over a rough striated surface. Maximum dimensions 27 by 23mm. Weight 13gm. Fill 3063 of ditch 3060 (Enclosure C), Period 4.3.
Folded and crumpled offcut lead sheet, with six layers in places. Maximum dimensions 49 by 39mm. Weight 31gm. Fill 2431 of posthole 2430 (Structure 6), Period 4.3.
Three lead amorphous dribbles. Total weight 37gm. Probably residual Roman. Unstratified.
Approximately 50 hobnails and fragments. Average length 11mm. Probably contemporary with the filling of the ditch rather than disturbed grave goods from an early burial, as the leather is unlikely to have survived until the later period. Fill 2472 of ditch 2365, Period 4.3.
Iron ?stylus fragment, slightly shouldered at one end. Length 59mm. Fill 2648 of ditch 2649, Period 4.1 to 4.3.

The Worked Bone, by Emma Harrison

Bone object with one end cut and bevelled (Fig. 19.1). Made from the left mid to distal shaft from a sheep/goat (bone identified by Lorrain Higbee). The distal end of the shaft bears canid gnaw marks. A groove has been worn around the bone 22mm from the unworked end. Polished surface. Possible handle or toggle. Length 65mm. Fill 2745 of ditch 2744 (n.i.), Period 4.3.

The Glass, by Emma Harrison

Ten small fragments of colourless and blue/green glass were recovered, nine of which are from vessels. The identifiable fragments include a base from a square bottle and a kick from a bottle base. Also recovered was a fragment with one prominent rib from a pillar moulded bowl. These bowls are common on 1st-century sites in Britain and the Roman Empire and, in blue/green glass, were in use until the end of the 1st century AD (Price and Cottam 1998, 73). The one fragment not from a vessel is a stirring rod. Stirring rods are also found on sites throughout the Empire, and the majority, like this example, have twisted stems (Allason-Jones and Miket 1984, 275). Similar examples from sites in Britain include South Shields Roman fort (ibid., 277, Fig. 4.7) and Fishbourne (Harden and Price 1971, Fig. 144.106–7).

Catalogue of illustrated glass objects (Fig. 19)

2. Blue/green stirring rod. Circular section with a twisted stem. One end is flattened and expanded into a disc; the other is broken. Length 22mm. Diameter of rod 6mm; diameter of head 12mm. Fill 3224 of ditch 3053 (Enclosure C), Period 4.3.

Non-illustrated glass objects

Blue/green fragment with one prominent rib, the front face of which has been broken off. From a pillar moulded bowl. Fill 3251 of pit 3250, Period 4.1.

Objects of Fired Clay, by Emma Harrison

Two small triangular loomweight fragments were recovered from Roman contexts. One, from pit 3374 (Period 4.1), has the perforation and one surviving flat face while the other, from posthole 2889 (Period 4.2), has two flat faces at right angles. Triangular loomweights can be Iron Age or early Roman in date (Barclay 1999, 421), and the former was found in association with 1st or 2nd-century pottery. The third fragment, from ditch 2985 (Period 4.3), has a curved surface and could possibly be from a loomweight or similar object, or be a fragment of pit lining. Also recovered were two fragments which join to form a hemisphere (Fig. 19.3). These are obviously part of a larger object of unknown shape and function.

Catalogue of illustrated fragments (Fig. 19)

3. Two joining fragments which form a hemisphere of diameter 40mm. Weight 33gm. Sandy fabric tempered with cut organic material. Fill 2375 of gully 2369, Period 4.2.
4. Mould fragments. See Metallurgical Residues (below).

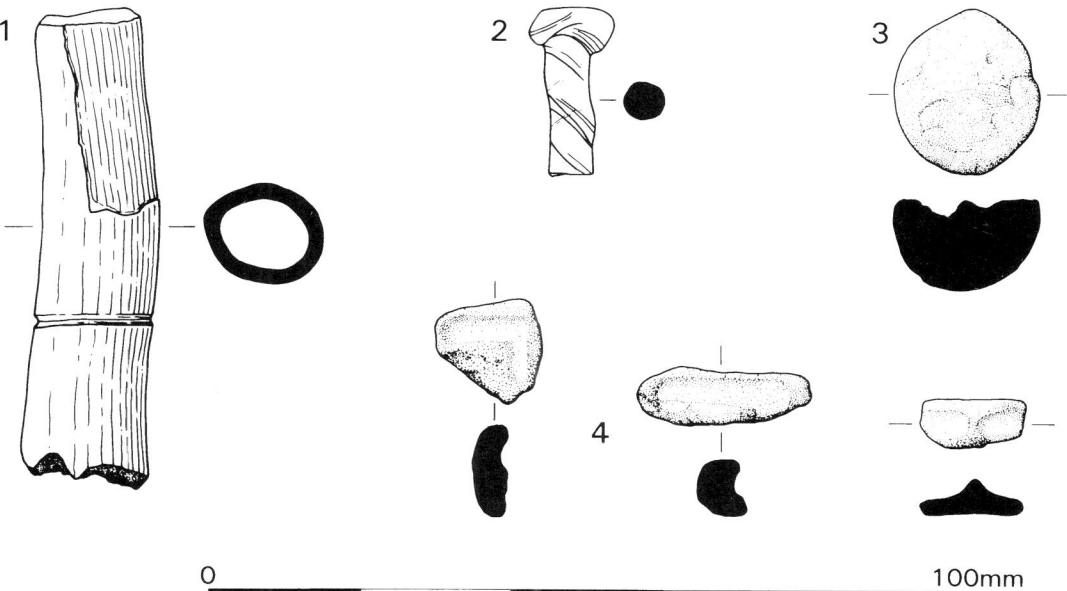

Fig. 19: Objects of bone, glass and fired clay (scale 1:1)

The Tile, by Emma Harrison

The majority of the tile consists of small, unidentifiable fragments. However, among the tile assemblage retrieved from Roman contexts, 16 fragments were identified as tegula, 16 as imbrex, and many of the unidentified fragments are also likely to be roof tile. Also recovered were two definite, and two possible, box-tile fragments. One of these was found intrusively in Period 3 roundhouse posthole 2173 (fill 2174), which had been severely truncated by a medieval plough furrow. It had been scored with a diagonal lattice pattern. Scoring of box tiles is less common than combing, and Brodribb (1989, 109) suggests that it might have been a precursor to the use of combs. Much of the tile was deposited in ditches, particularly those at the southern end of the area of Roman occupation. The majority of the tile was retrieved from Period 4.3 features, with very little from Period 4.2 and almost none from Period 4.1.

The Worked Stone, by Fiona Roe

The assemblage is divided into two groups: objects and building stone, with the objects further divided by date into prehistoric and Roman material.

Late Bronze Age/Early-Middle Iron Age objects

A fragment of May Hill sandstone from posthole 2167 in Structure 1 may have been used as post packing. May Hill sandstone was extensively traded, possibly without a break, from the Neolithic until the Middle Iron Age. At the time of writing, 19 Gloucestershire Iron Age sites with querns of this material are known, but Bronze Age sites have so far escaped identification in the county. The majority of the recorded sites are of Middle Iron Age date, but three earlier local sites provide a precedent for the find from the Link Road: Irely Farm, Stanway (Saville 1984, 171); Shenberrow Hill Camp, Stanton (Fell 1961, 31); and Crickley Hill (Philip Dixon, pers. comm.).

Burnt stone is a common feature at sites of this general date, and the two fragments of burnt quartzite may belong to this period, although one came from Roman midden 2848 and the second from Burial 14.

Catalogue (not illustrated)

Weathered piece of stone, now without working traces, but a saddle quern material; May Hill Sandstone. Dimensions 106mm x 69.5mm x 42.5mm; weight 217g. Fill 2168 of posthole 2167 (Structure 1), Period 3.

Roman objects

A fine-grained sandstone pebble possibly collected from a local Pleistocene river terrace deposit (Green 1992, 158), was identified as a whetstone. The quartzite pebble used as a polisher could have come from a similar source. This polisher is only slightly worn, but similar quartzite pebbles, well worn to a glossy surface, are relatively common on Roman sites and may be pot burnishers. Examples from Gloucestershire include Kingscote; Wortley Roman villa (Taylor and Bagnall 1993, 34, Fig. 15.284); Home Farm, Bishop's Cleeve (Roe 1998, 130); and Birdlip Quarry, Cowley (Roe 1999, 419).

The small fragment of Niedermendig lava from midden 2848 no longer retains working traces. Lava is quite common on Gloucestershire Roman sites, occurring at both Gloucester and Cirencester, and another nine sites. It was used both for millstones, as at Wortley Roman villa (Taylor and Bagnall 1989, 43, Fig. 14.121), and for rotary querns of the Roman disc type, as for instance an unstratified find at Birdlip Quarry, Cowley (Roe 1999, 416). Dating is for the most part somewhat uncertain.

Catalogue (not illustrated)

Whetstone. Flat waterworn pebble with two main areas of wear along the edges and three smaller facets; fine-grained green-grey siltstone or mudstone. Dimensions 78mm x 56mm x 15.5mm; weight 100g. Unstratified.
Polisher. Pebble with large chip missing from one end, slight traces of shiny surface from use; quartzite. Dimensions 115mm x 81.5mm x 57mm; weight 699g. Fill 2543 of gully 2542, Period 4.2.
Quern or millstone. Weathered fragment without working traces; Niedermendig lava. Dimensions 121mm x 65.5mm x 44.5mm; weight 381g. Fill 2975 of midden 2848, Period 4.3.

Roman building stone

Local Jurassic limestone and Old Red Sandstone, from the Cotswolds and Forest of Dean respectively, were used as building materials, but the amounts are relatively small, and were well scattered over the site. Most of the stone was retrieved from ditches, with usually only one or two items per ditch. Period 4.3 accounts for most of the building material, with *c.* 12kg of tile and paving and *c.* 4.6kg of building stone.

Local Jurassic limestone, which was probably used as structural material, came from only five contexts, and amounts to just 4.8kg. It can be assumed that any good building blocks would have been long since reused. A rather coarse-grained, shelly oolitic limestone, probably from the Great Oolite, appears to have been the main variety of building stone, but shell fragmental limestone from the Great Oolite and oolitic limestone, probably Lower Freestone from the Inferior Oolite, were also used. All of this stone was available within a few kilometres of the site. Apart from its use in Gloucester (Hunter 1963, 64), similar limestone was used for building at the nearby Hucclecote Roman villa (Clifford 1933, 329; Williams 1971, 100) and other sites in the vicinity such as Brockworth (Rawes 1981, 73) and Great Witcombe (Clifford 1954, 24; Leach 1998, 97). Local Jurassic limestone was also utilised at Birdlip Quarry, Cowley (Roe 1999, 419).

The greater part of the building material consists of Old Red Sandstone, probably the Lower Old Red Sandstone Brownstones in the Forest of Dean. Fragments with a hole drilled through, found in fills 2285 and 2472 of ditch 2365 (Period 4.3), along with one of typical hexagonal shape, also found in 2285, attest to its use as roofing tile. Pieces with thickness of up to *c.* 30mm were used. Only one fragment of limestone roofing tile was found. Paving of sandstone was identified by worn surfaces and generally more substantial thicknesses of up to 49mm. There seems to have been a preference for buff-coloured stone for paving, rather than the red sandstone used for roofing. A little local Lias was also used for paving stone.

Old Red Sandstone (Brownstones) was also used for roofing in Gloucester (Hunter 1963, 64), and was probably transported by boat from the Forest of Dean. Its further distribution was restricted largely to sites within convenient reach, such as Hucclecote (Clifford 1933, 329), Barnwood (Rawes 1977, 31), Brockworth (Rawes 1981, 73) and Great Witcombe (Clifford 1954, 24; Leach 1998, 94), but not further east where Jurassic limestone is more common (e.g. Birdlip Quarry, Cowley and Vineyards Farm, Charlton Kings) although the latter yielded a little Old Red Sandstone (Rawes 1991, 55). The finds from the Link Road show that the stone used for building was typical of sites within the immediate area.

The Worked Flint, by Graeme Walker

Nineteen pieces of worked flint were recovered. The small assemblage contains artefacts worked from a variety of raw material sources ranging from good quality black and grey flint to slightly poorer quality mottled grey flint. Typically for the region the assemblage is dominated by small pieces, and the only core present is also very small, indicating the maximisation of product from a scarce, imported resource. The largest pieces are only present in the very best quality flint, and there is no primary flaking waste present, again typical of imported material.

The overall condition of the assemblage is very good. The fresh appearance of much of the material indicates that it has not been greatly reworked, and breakages, where present, would appear to have occurred in antiquity. Traces of edge utilisation on some flakes are clearly distinguishable. Some patination is present on a few pieces.

A large 'thumbnail-like' scraper and a segment of a possible broken knife might indicate a Bronze Age date, while an obliquely-blunted microlith indicates a Mesolithic component. The microlith and four flakes were recovered from postholes within Structure 1 which is broadly dated by pottery to the late Bronze Age or early Iron Age. The remainder of the assemblage was recovered from Romano-British contexts. The concentration of artefacts towards the northern end of the site is more likely to reflect recovery bias than a significant distribution.

Metallurgical Residues and Related Materials, by Tim Young and Helen S. Bowstead Stallybrass

Small quantities of material from pyrotechnical processes were recovered from a wide range of contexts. The dominant material is a grey, glassy, vesicular slag which occurs in contexts from Period 3 (2165, 2189) and Period 4 (1010, 2631, 2889, 2932, 2985, 3238). Crucible fragments were recovered from two Period 4 contexts (2905 and 3273). Also recovered from pit 3273 were fragments of hearth lining and moulds.

Grey glassy, vesicular slags, by Tim Young

These vesicular slags are of the kind sometimes referred to as 'fluxed lining slags' (Crew 1996). However, they may have an origin in various processes, not only as the product of fluxing of the hearth lining by the fuel ash in a metallurgical hearth (either ferrous or non-ferrous), but in various other sorts of hearths and ovens, or even during accidental burning of clay-rich materials. It is therefore possible that the material in these various contexts does not derive from the same process, despite the similarity of the residues.

Most of the fragments are rather small (these slags are very fragile), but posthole 2889 (Period 4.2) yielded a significant quantity of larger pieces. This sample was analysed for major element composition and selected trace metals (details in the site archive). The analytical procedures were intended to reveal any evidence of metallurgical processes. Such indications might come from the chemical composition (raised proportion of iron, or non-ferrous metals) or from textural studies (traces of included hammerscale or blebs of metal).

The content of the economic metals and associated elements (Fe, Cr, Cu, Zn, As, Mo, Pb) is all very low, and within the range of subsoil clays. There is therefore no evidence for the input of metals to these samples from metallurgical processes. It is worth noting that the levels of As and Mo are relatively low, and these elements typically show a high degree of enrichment when coal is employed as fuel. That possibility (raised in the initial evaluation of this material) can therefore be discounted. The sample was also subject to investigation by scanning electron microscope (SEM). It is highly vesicular, with the vesicles ranging from a few microns up to several millimetres. The slag phase bears quartz grains of up to 500 microns in a groundmass which is predominantly glass, but which shows a significant degree of crystallisation. Details of the SEM analysis can be found in the archive.

There are very few detailed descriptions of slags like these in the literature, probably because they are generally considered to be non-diagnostic. However, study of similar materials from other sites has shown that small pieces of hammerscale can usually be seen in slags like these where they are associated with blacksmithing. This was not the case with the material examined here. If the material had been associated with the working of non-ferrous materials, then equally a small amount of contamination of the hearth residues by the metal might be expected, but again this is not evident in this material. Casting of non-ferrous metals can produce minimal contamination of the hearth, for the metal is enclosed in a crucible, and there is no means for the positive identification of such an activity from the hearth residues in the absence of crucible or mould fragments.

Crucibles and hearth lining, by Tim Young

Two crucible fragments from pits 2905 (Period 4.3) and 3273 (Period 4.1) were carbon coated and mounted for SEM examination. One specimen of probable hearth lining also from pit 3273 was also examined.

Two analyses of the unaltered crucible ceramic of the crucible base (3273) were conducted with different specimen orientation, but show remarkably similar compositions (24–25% Al_2O_3, 58–59% SiO_2, 2–3% K_2O, 1% CaO, 2% MgO). The aluminium content seems reasonably high (25% is the minimum Al_2O_3 content for a fireclay), but if the alkalis are a primary component of the ceramic then they would have reduced the softening temperature considerably. The slag material is more aluminous (relative to the silica content) than the ceramic, slightly enriched in iron, and strongly enriched in calcium and phosphorus. The non-ferrous metal content of the slag includes up to 3.4% Cu expressed as CuO and up to 30% Sn expressed as SnO. The high tin:copper ratio is commonly seen in slags of this nature, and appears to reflect the preferential leaching of copper in post-depositional alteration, rather than being an indication that the crucible was used for metallic tin.

The crucible rim (2905) shows a very different suite of analyses. The surface of the rim, and the upper part of the vesicular material inside (probably itself mainly melted crucible rather than a separate slag phase) show elevated iron contents (equivalent to 29–54% FeO). It is unlikely that such iron-rich material comprises a great thickness, but none the less, the levels are extremely high. Within the thickness of the vesicular material the iron contents fall rapidly to close to those observed in the body of the crucible fragments from pit 3273 (5–6% FeO). Phosphorus and calcium show irregular enrichment within the vesicular material, presumably reflecting reaction with the fuel.

An elevated iron content in some slags from copper-alloy working has been noted previously (Tylecote 1986), and has been related to the iron content of the copper, deliberate use of iron oxides as a flux to clean the metal, or to the use of iron tools for manipulating the crucible. In this case, the significance of the iron-rich slag is uncertain, but it appears to form only a very thin veneer on the crucible.

The piece of probable hearth lining has a reddish, oxidised fabric, with an extremely vesicular surficial layer a few millimetres thick. Analyses of the fabric and vesicular layer include several clustering around Al_2O_3 of 24%, SiO_2 of 60%, CaO <1% and K_2O of 2–5%. These indicate a clay of broadly similar composition to that of the crucible. As with the crucible slags the clay shows substantial fluxing by the fuel ash with Ca and P both markedly enriched in spots 3, 6 and 8. The same spots show enrichment of iron, providing some suggestion that the piece is from an iron-working hearth, but as noted above local enrichment of iron is possible under other circumstances, so identification of iron working on the basis of this one fragment would be premature. It is interesting that the crucible fragments do not seem to be accompanied by the glassy slags seen in the other phases.

Moulds, by Helen S. Bowstead Stallybrass

Mould fragments weighing *c.* 100g were recovered from the fill 3274 of pit 3273, Period 4.1 (Fig. 19.4). They appear to be from investment (lost wax) moulds.

Methodology

Following the careful examination of all the fragments, their surfaces were analysed non-quantitatively by x-ray fluorescence (XRF) analysis to identify the types of metal with which they had been in contact. XRF is a non-destructive technique. It works on the principle that every element will generate its own slightly different characteristic x-rays when bombarded with x-rays from a source. By identifying these characteristic secondary x-rays, elements present within a material can be identified. However, quantitative analysis of material is difficult by this method due to a number of factors.

The proportions of metals found within moulds is dependent both on the original composition of the melt and the metals' chemical nature. Elements such as zinc are very volatile and so diffuse into the mould walls (Bayley 1992, 817–18). When analysed it is well represented even if originally it only formed a very small part of the melted metal (Barnes, no date). Analysis of moulds can be difficult, and often, even when a mould has been used for casting, no trace of metal is detected. This is due to the relatively short period of time that the mould is in contact with a molten metal (Wilthew *et al.* 1991, 142).

Results

The moulds are made of one clay fabric which is very fine-grained, organic inclusions having burned out when the mould was fired. Some of the moulds are also tempered with coarse grains of sandstone with diameter between 1mm and 2mm. The inclusions are found throughout the moulds and can be seen on both the inner and outer surfaces.

No metals were detected on any of the mould surfaces. This means that no positive identification of any alloys that may have been worked can be achieved.

The 33 mould fragments from the site are of mixed quality. Two identifiable fragments survive from sprue cups, an integral part of an investment mould. The other fragments are also thought to be from investment moulds, but no diagnostic detail survives. Consequently no conclusions can be drawn as to what objects had been cast in the moulds. All the mould fragments are partially reduced fired (near the inner surfaces) and partially oxidised fired; typical firing patterns of clay moulds that have been used. The lack of metals on the mould surfaces shows that a skilled craftsman was at work.

Discussion
The analysis of the vesicular slags showed neither enhancement in metal content, nor any textures suggestive of incorporation of metallic blebs or particles. These slags might have an origin in a process where metal is confined to a crucible (i.e. non-ferrous metal casting), but could equally have an origin in any process where clay, including the local soil or subsoil, came into contact with a fire and was heated to temperatures in excess of approximately 900° C. This would not be normal in a domestic hearth, but is possible, intentionally or otherwise, in a wide variety of situations.

One of the crucible fragments (3273) provides good analytical data to show it was used for handling a tin bronze. However, the second crucible fragment (2905; Period 4.3) and a fragment of hearth lining (also from pit 3273) do not reveal contamination from the metal, but do show elevated iron contents. The significance of this is uncertain, as iron itself could not have been worked in the crucible. It is also of note that the crucible fragments are apparently not accompanied by the glassy slags seen in the other phases, perhaps suggesting that these materials are being produced through different and unrelated processes.

The moulds provide additional evidence that non-ferrous metalworking occurred on the site. Although much of the collection is heavily abraded, it is potentially an important group of material. It is difficult to establish the type of objects that have been cast on this site due to the poor surface survival of the moulds. Although no analytical identification of the metal cast in the moulds was possible, comparison with other similar metalworking sites such as Gussage All Saints, Dorset (Spratling 1979) or Weelsby Avenue, Grimsby (Foster 1995) suggests that the moulds were probably used for casting bronze. It is unlikely that production on the scale of Gussage All Saints or Weelsby Avenue, where several thousand mould fragments were found (Foster 1995, 58), was occurring, as only a maximum of 31 moulds survive. It is more likely that production was on a similar scale to that occurring at Beckford, Worcestershire where a smaller number of moulds was found (Hurst and Wills 1987). It is likely that these finds are in their original dumping place as the material is confined to one deposit within one pit. This follows similar patterns at Gussage All Saints and Weelsby Avenue where the majority of finds were found in one location (Spratling 1979, 125–8; Foster 1995, 49). The moulds are typical of Late Iron Age moulds and, if Romano-British in date, indicate a continuation of native craftsmanship rather than a switch to more typical Romano-British piece moulds.

THE BIOLOGICAL EVIDENCE

The Human Remains, by Tony Waldron

The human remains consisted of three cremations and thirteen inhumations. Detailed information on each burial is provided in the grave catalogues within the Excavation Results section (above).

The Cremations

The cremations (Burials 1, 5 and 8) were all of a similar texture and colour and all were of adults. Burial 1, which was considerably larger than the other two, was sieved after recovery; the other two were not sieved. The fragments tended to be rather small in size, suggesting that the bones had been crushed after cremation, and it is evident from the weights of the fragments that all represented only a sample of the cremated remains rather than the whole. This is reinforced by the fact that no teeth were present in any of the cremations.

The small size of the fragments meant that very few pieces could be positively identified, and although it was clear that all the cremations were of adults, neither sex nor age could be determined. There were no signs of pathology in any of the remains. The main features of each of the cremations are shown in Table 6.

Table 6: Characteristics of the cremations

Burial	Colour	Weight (g)		Size (mm)		Identified elements	Positive identifications
		2-11.2mm	>11.2mm	Minimum	Maximum		
1	Grey/white	1351	440	c. 1	49	Skull, long bone fragments, vertebral fragments	1 metatarsal head; upper articulation of talus; tibial tuberosity; distal articulation of humerus
5	Grey/white	148		<1	19	All unidentified	None
8	Grey/white	c.4		<1	8	All unidentified	None

The Inhumations

The inhumations were generally substantially complete, but they had suffered considerable post-mortem damage which limited the amount of information that could be derived from them. Where possible each skeleton was assigned an age and sex, and measurements were taken to calculate height, using the equations published by Mildred Trotter (1970), or to calculate femoral or tibial indices. Evidence of any pathology was noted and assigned to most probable cause.

Of the thirteen inhumations, two were definitely male; nine were female and sex could not be assigned to the remaining two. The age range was considerable; two of the females were aged between 15 and 25 at the time of their death; one was between 25 and 35, one between 35 and 45, and the remaining five females were all at least 45 when they died. One of the males was aged between 15 and 25, while it was not possible to give an age to the other male skeleton or to one of those of unknown sex, although both were adults; the final skeleton was between 35 and 45 when he or she died. The salient features of each of the skeletons are summarised in Table 7. Age and sex were determined using standard anthropological techniques (WEA 1980).

Many of the skeletons had signs of pathology, and there was one extremely interesting case of mesomelic dyschondroplasia which is discussed in more detail in the grave catalogue.

Table 7: Characteristics of the inhumations
OA = osteoarthritis; SCJ = sternoclavicular joint

Burial	Sex	Age	Height (m)	Femoral index	Tibial index	Pathology
2	Unknown	35-45				Enamel hypoplasia, dental caries
3	Male	15-25	1.53	79.4 (l) 83.3 (r)	85.7 (r)	Dyschondroseosis
4	Female	35-45			70.0	OA spine
6	Female	45 +		73.5		OA hands and spine; infective arthropathy of right wrist; enamel hypoplasia; dental caries
7	Female	45 +	1.63		74.3	OA right knee, left hip, spine, right hand and elbow, right SCJ; ante-mortem tooth
9	Female	45 +	1.53	74.0	77.4	OA hand, right SJC; lumbar degenerative disc disease, Schmorls' nodes; ante-mortem tooth loss
10	Unknown	Adult				
11	Female	25-35	1.59	77.4	67.7	Lumbar disc disease
12	Female	15-25		83.1		Dental caries
13	Female	45 +	1.59	68.8		OA right elbow, both wrists and hands; dental caries
14	Male	Adult				Cervical disc disease; ante-mortem tooth loss
15	Female	15-25		71.9		
16	Female	45 +		80.0		Lumbar disc disease

Animal Bone, by Tracey Stickler

Of the 2090 specimens recorded in the archive, 1845 are from datable contexts, and 670 of these have been identified to species. The bulk of faunal material was derived from Romano-British deposits (Periods 4.1–3), but small amounts of prehistoric, medieval and 18th-century material were briefly noted. Horse, cattle, sheep and pig are all well represented, and there are small quantities of red and roe deer, dog, goat and bird. An articulated dog skeleton was recovered from 2936 (Period 4.3 midden), an articulated horse limb from Enclosure C ditch 3044 (Period 4.3), and a leg of lamb from Burial 12. The assemblage is well preserved, there is evidence for butchery, and two cases of pathology are presented.

Methods

The comparative collection of T.D. Stickler was used to aid identification. Where possible specimens were recorded to species and anatomy, while undiagnostic fragments were assigned to the following classes: large (horse, cattle, red deer), medium (sheep/goat, roe deer, pig), small (dog, cat, hare), very small (rodent, amphibian) or unidentifiable. For each specimen a subjective assessment of condition was recorded, along with details of fragmentation, butchery, epiphysial fusion and pathology. Tooth wear was recorded after Grant (1982), and tooth measurements taken. Measurements of whole and mature bone specimens, taken using vernier callipers, were recorded in millimetres after the methods of von den Driesch (1976). Proportions of long bone proximal and distal elements are included in calculations of the minimum number of individuals (MNI), and handedness is adjusted for. Withers heights were calculated using formula collated by von den Driesch and Boessneck (1974).

Table 8: Animal bones from Romano-British deposits
NISP = no. of identified specimans (fragments). MNI = minimum number of individuals

Element	Horse	Cattle	Red deer	other large	Roe deer	Sheep/ goat	Goat	Pig	other medium	Dog	other small	Total
Horn core/antler	-	-	-	-	-	-	1	-	-	-	-	1
Cranial	-	10	1	16	-	-	-	14	-	-	-	41
Mandible	-	16	4	19	1	26	-	5	-	1	3	75
Atlas	-	2	-	-	-	-	-	-	-	-	-	2
Axis	-	-	-	1	-	-	-	-	-	-	1	2
Cervical vert.	-	4	-	2	-	1	-	-	-	-	-	7
Thoracic vert.	-	6	-	1	-	1	-	-	-	2	1	11
Rib	1	7	-	7	-	1	-	-	-	-	11	27
Lumbar vert.	-	-	1	1	-	-	-	-	-	-	-	2
Scapula	-	13	-	1	-	3	-	-	-	-	2	19
Humerus	1	5	-	1	-	2	-	-	-	-	6	15
Radius	1	-	-	-	-	3	-	-	-	-	8	12
Ulna	-	-	-	-	1	3	-	-	-	-	3	7
Carpal	-	2	-	1	-	1	-	-	-	-	-	4
Metacarpal	1	8	-	-	-	12	-	-	-	-	-	21
Inominate	-	3	-	2	-	3	-	-	1	-	3	12
Femur	-	3	1	1	-	3	-	-	-	-	10	18
Tibia	5	6	-	1	-	7	-	-	-	-	11	30
Fibula	-	1	-	-	-	-	-	-	-	-	-	1
Tarsal	2	14	-	-	-	1	-	-	-	-	-	17
Metarsal	2	9	-	-	1	9	-	-	1	-	-	22
Sesamoid	-	1	-	-	-	-	-	-	-	-	-	1
1st Phalange	-	6	-	-	-	3	-	-	-	-	-	9
2nd Phalange	-	2	-	-	-	-	-	-	-	-	-	2
3rd Phalange	-	-	-	-	-	2	-	-	-	-	-	2
Diagnostic	13	118	7	54	3	81	1	19	2	3	59	360
Teeth	12	28	-	-	-	56	-	5	-	-	-	101
Unidentified	-	-	-	27	-	-	-	-	-	-	2	29
Articulated	15	-	-	-	-	8	-	-	-	107	-	130
Bird bones	-	-	-	-	-	-	-	-	-	-	-	3
NISP	40	146	7	81	3	145	1	24	2	110	61	623
MNI	1	4	1	1	1	2	1	2	1	2	1	

Results

Prehistoric deposits (Periods 2–3) produced 198 specimens primarily comprising small, poorly preserved and undiagnostic fragments, some of which had been burned. Of the ten specimens identified, cattle are represented by two loose teeth; dog by two measurable mandibles (both suggest an age of about one year and are probably from the same animal); sheep by portions of mandible and tibia, and a loose tooth; and pig by a portion of tibia and a loose tooth. The remaining specimen is from a very small mammal. There is no evidence of green fragmentation (the purposeful breaking of a bone while still wet) or butchery.

The Romano-British deposits (Periods 4.1–3; Table 8) produced 1617 specimens, 623 of which have been identified to species and comprise: 101 loose teeth; 130 specimens from the articulated deposits; 360 individual specimens identifiable to element; and 29 undiagnostic fragments assigned as small (2) or large (27). Evidence of weathering and butchery are minimal at 2% each, 3% of specimens appear to have been gnawed, 11% of specimens have been heated and 16% display green fractures.

It is evident from Table 9 that cattle and sheep occur in similar amounts in the Roman periods. When values are adjusted for the likelihood that the vast majority of large specimens are derived from cattle, and similarly medium from sheep (Table 10), cattle are better represented. Loose teeth were recovered from cattle, horse, sheep, and pig. In 16% of the sheep, and 3.5% of the cattle, teeth are deciduous, while none of the horse or pig are deciduous. Tooth wear score distribution suggests that 70% of evaluated sheep teeth came from mature animals, cattle of all ages were equally represented, and pig teeth were only representative of young animals.

Table 9: *Representation of species in Romano-British deposits*

Species	Percentage
Horse	8
Cattle	29
Deer	2
Large	18
Sheep	30
Pig	3
Medium	<1
Dog	<1
Small	9

Table 10: *Adjusted proportional representations of cattle and sheep in Romano-British deposits*

Species	Percentage
Cattle	29
Large	18
Total probable cattle	**47**
Sheep	30
Medium	<1
Total probable sheep	**30**

Immature sheep in the local population are also indicated by unfused epiphyses, seven specimens suggest ages from 2.5–3.5 years, one an animal about ten months old, one a natal specimen, and the articulated leg from Burial 12 an animal of about one year old. Two specimens of unfused proximal horse tibia suggest animals of 3–3.5 years of age, while unfused vertebrae indicated immature dog, ox and red deer.

Thirty-six bone specimens from the Romano-British deposits provided measurable material. Apart from the reconstructed horse metacarpus discussed below, the elements represented cannot reliably be used to extrapolate animal size, and the small sample sizes means that statistical comparison with values obtained from other sites is of dubious significance.

Butchery evidence is more prevalent in specimens from Period 4.3 than the preceding two periods, and indicates processing of cattle, sheep, horse and bird. The butchery undertaken includes removal of breast meat from the bird, and marks on cattle specimens indicate the removal of lower limb portions with disarticulating chops, and upper forelimb meat removal with knife cuts. Sheep specimens suggest in one animal the removal of the hind limb from the pelvic girdle by means of heavy chopping around the joint, while in another the thoracic vertebrae are cleaved in half longitudinally. There is also evidence of lower limb removal by chopping through the knee. One unidentified medium and one small specimen also indicate disarticulation of the hip joint by chopping, whereas one large unidentified specimen indicates the removal of the head by chopping through the axis.

Articulated deposits

Three articulated deposits were recovered from Romano-British features. A dog grave (2936) from Period 4.3 midden 2848, contained 107 poorly preserved specimens from a mature animal. Some of the ribs and vertebrate are partly burnt, as are the right femur and tibia. Both tibia also display the slight curvature associated with small breeds of dog. In general the specimens were too damaged for measurements to be taken, but a single radius gave a length of 65mm. This suggests a withers height of 210mm (after Koudelka 1885 cited in von den Driesch and Boessneck 1974) or 226mm after Harcourt (1974), both measurements suggesting a small terrier sized animal. Deposited with Burial 12 was an uncooked, articulated leg of lamb, presumably an offering. One of the fills 3150 of the Enclosure C boundary ditch (Period 4.3) contained the articulated foreleg of a mature horse. All 15 specimens show signs of having been heated. Damage prevents full measurements being taken, but a reconstructed metacarpus gives a length of 233mm suggesting a withers height of 15 HH (149cm), a good sized horse (after Kiesewalter 1888 cited in von den Driesch and Boessneck 1974), more typical of the type introduced by the incoming Romans than a native pony.

Pathology

Two instances of unrelated pathology are represented. From gully 2369 (Period 4.2) a portion of a right cattle innominate, displaying a polished secondary articulating surface away from the acetabulum, was recovered. This was situated within a considerable mass of new bone, deposited in response to a broken hip and infection, and accommodated the proximal end of the displaced femur shaft, the head having been broken off. The animal would have experienced a reduced range of movement within this reactive joint and considerable pain, but the polish indicates its limited success as a replacement for the dysfunctional hip joint. An unphased Romano-British feature 2649 produced a right proximal bovine metatarsal displaying advanced arthritis of the hock.

Discussion

Little can be reliably interpreted from the small amount of prehistoric material, beyond the fact that the three main domesticates and dog are present.

The anatomical representation and the butchery associations of the Romano-British periods indicate that whole carcasses were present on site. The site is shown to have maintained breeding stock of cattle and sheep. A current hypothesis is that more Romanised sites exhibit an increased utilisation of cattle at the expense of both sheep and pig throughout the Roman period. This is a manifestation of the agricultural economy responding to cultural changes influencing the dietary requirements of the local population. The adjusted representation of cattle at the Link Road site is 47% compared to 30% for sheep. The small terrier sized dog recovered from the Period 4.3 midden falls outside Harcourt's range for Roman dogs (Harcourt 1974), but a similar sized Roman animal was recovered from The Beeches Nursery Field, Cirencester (O'Connor 1990).

The Plant Remains, by Alan Thomas

Twelve bulk samples were taken from the excavation: six from Middle Bronze Age cremations and features; one from Late Bronze Age/Early Iron Age pit 2420; four from Romano-British features, and one from undated pit 2235. Full details can be found in the site archive. The samples were all heavily contaminated by modern roots, and most of the samples contained modern weed seeds. Charred cereal grains were rare, occurring in cremation Burials 1 and 5 (Period 2), and Burial 4 (Period 4.3). Charred weed seeds were also found in Structure 3 posthole 2189 (Period 3), Burial 7 and midden 2848 (Period 4.3). Two charred spikelet forks were also retrieved from the sample from Burial 4 (Period 4.3). The occurrence of small numbers of charred cereal grains and charred weed seeds in some of the samples suggests a partially processed cereal product that was probably discarded as rubbish from domestic activity.

DISCUSSION, BY NEIL HOLBROOK

The excavations in advance of the construction of the Link Road have examined a transect through a complex and long-lived archaeological site. Inevitably the restricted area available for excavation hampers overall considerations of spatial patterning, although the geophysical surveys do at least provide some indication of the complexity of features that lie beyond the road corridor, and of the overall extent of the site.

The prehistoric evidence

The identification of up to 2m of alluvium which had been deposited by the Horsbere Brook prior to the establishment of the Middle Bronze Age cremation cemetery is of considerable interest. The most likely source of material to form this alluvium is soil washed from the surfaces of cultivated fields, which in itself is indicative of land clearance and agricultural activity on the Cotswold escarpment and higher reaches of the Horsbere Brook. This complements the environmental work at other locations in the Severn Valley which suggests that deforestation of the valley floor was underway by the Early Bronze Age, and that the process was actively ongoing into the first millennium BC. Pollen evidence from the Ripple Brook, just to the north of Tewkesbury, suggests that between 1000–400 BC the vegetational character of this area changed from being heavily wooded to one that was cleared and intensively farmed (Brown and Barber 1985). In this part of the Severn Valley to the east of Gloucester intensive agriculture was clearly being undertaken before the 14th to 12th century BC to judge from the radiocarbon dates from Burial 1. Similarly the gravel terrace around Frocester, 17km further south in the Vale, displays an intensification of activity from the Middle Bronze Age (Darvill 2000, 239), a pattern also found on the lias clays near Tewkesbury (Walker *et al.* forthcoming).

The earliest ceramics from the site comprise an isolated sherd of Early Bronze Age beaker. No features could be attributed to this period, and a background scatter of such pottery frequently occurs on later sites in the area. A beaker burial accompanied by a complete vessel was excavated at Barnwood, 2km to the west, in the 1920s (Clifford 1930, Fig. 7).

The Middle Bronze Age cremations appear to belong to a flat cemetery: it is very unlikely that they were covered with mounds given that their sites were reused for Late Bronze Age/Early Iron Age settlement. The tradition of internment in round barrows began to decline from about 1200 BC to be replaced by flat cremation cemeteries such as are found over much of southern Britain. Little can be said about the layout of the cemetery, given the relatively narrow area investigated, and indeed it is possible that the cremations represent secondary internments around an earlier barrow that lay outside the excavated area (as at Bevan's Quarry, Temple Guiting; O'Neil 1967). The isolated, undated, crouched inhumation Burial 2 might date to the later Prehistoric period. Tightly crouched burials within flat graves are characteristic of the Later Bronze Age (Barratt *et al.* 1991, 214) and have been found at two sites within the Upper Thames Valley in Gloucestershire. At Shorncote, near Cirencester, two inhumations associated with urned and unurned cremations yielded radiocarbon dates of 1520–1370 or 1350–1310 cal. BC and 1445–1120 cal. BC (Barclay and Glass 1995, 49), while a similar burial at Roughground Farm near Lechlade yielded a date of 1310–820 cal. BC (Allen *et al.* 1993, 35, 45). Such burials can also be of later date, as the isolated Middle Iron Age inhumations from Baunton, near Cirencester, and Burial 18 at Frocester, amply demonstrate (Mudd *et al.* 1999, vol. 1, 76; Price 2000, vol. 2, 208). The settlement to which the burials relate might not have been too far distant, for Bradley (1981,

101) has demonstrated that Middle Bronze Age Deverel-Rimbury style cremation cemeteries were typically situated close to settlements. Indeed Middle Bronze Age activity is recorded from beneath Hucclecote Roman villa, 650m distant, although little can be said of its nature (Clifford 1933, 331–2; Darvill 1987, 112).

The site of the cremation cemetery was subsequently adopted for a settlement which comprised at least four or five post-built roundhouses. Further structures doubtless lay beyond the excavated area. Charcoal associated with one of the roundhouses yielded a radiocarbon date of 787–399 cal. BC, while that from a small pit within Structure 1/3 produced dates of 760–385 cal. BC and 761–262 cal. BC. The pottery provides little differentiation save a broad Late Bronze Age/Early Iron Age date. The tradition of post-built roundhouses is recorded in the Late Bronze Age at Shorncote (Hearne and Heaton 1994, 49; Hearne and Adam 1999, 45–50) and in the early Iron Age at Crickley Hill (Dixon 1973). A post-built roundhouse (Structure 4) has also been excavated within the Middle-Late Iron Age enclosure at Frocester (Price 2000, vol.1, 51). The discovery of a Late Bronze Age/Early Iron Age domestic settlement within the Severn Valley is a welcome addition to our knowledge of this area, for non-hillfort sites are currently very poorly represented. There was activity at Frocester from the Late Bronze Age, and a Middle Iron Age palisaded settlement has been examined (Price 2000, vol. 1, 43–51). Elsewhere in the Vale evidence of Early Iron Age activity is often dependent upon stray finds of pottery, as at Gloucester (Dunning 1933) and Charlton Kings (Purnell and Webb 1950). The sherd of Middle Iron Age pottery from an isolated feature at the Link Road suggests that activity of this date occurred in the vicinity of the excavated area.

The Romano-British evidence

It must remain an open question whether there was late pre-Roman Iron Age occupation at the Link Road, or whether the site was newly established in the first decade or so following the Roman invasion of AD 43. An immediate pre-Conquest phase would be ceramically indistinguishable from a post-Conquest assemblage that contains only a mixture of native wares and early Severn Valley types (Timby 1990), although Timby (see above) tentatively suggests that the high proportion of these wares in Period 4.1 at least raises the possibility of pre-Conquest occupation. It is also of note that Period 4.1 deposits yielded a non-ferrous metalworking mould which is typologically of Late Iron Age type, and a fragment of Late Iron Age/Early Roman loomweight. It is unlikely that we will be able to determine whether there was a pre-existing farmstead at the time of the establishment of a legionary fortress at Kingsholm in the years following c. AD 48/9, or whether the farm developed in the immediate aftermath of that event as part of the process of agricultural intensification concerned with military supply, be it officially driven or locally inspired.

The Period 4.1 settlement was doubtless primarily concerned with food production, similar to the farmstead at nearby Brockworth (Rawes 1981) (Fig. 1). It contained at least three roundhouses to judge from the lengths of curving gully found; the restored diameters of 11–12m are certainly consistent with this interpretation. Comparison can be made with the two late 1st-century roundhouses excavated at Brockworth (diameters 10.5m and 8.6m; Rawes 1981, 48) and that at Abbeymead Roman Fields (Atkin 1987, 14–15). It was suggested that a late Iron Age roundhouse at Abbeydale Saintbridge was built of turf to judge from the lack of evidence for timber posts (Atkin 1987, 12), an occurrence also noted at Brockworth, Tewkesbury (Walker *et al.* forthcoming) and the present site. It is thus likely that there was a tradition of mass-walled roundhouse construction in the Severn Valley in the Late Iron Age/Early Roman periods.

The Link Road site can be compared with a growing number of agricultural settlements in the hinterland of Gloucester that have produced mid 1st-century pottery assemblages (Fig. 1). At Abbeymead Roman Fields a Late Iron Age roundhouse was replaced by a Romano-British field system associated with a new roundhouse which dates to the mid 1st–mid 2nd century (Atkin 1987, 14–15). At Abbeydale Saintbridge Late Iron Age ditched enclosures (possibly surrounding roundhouses) were replaced in the mid 1st-mid 2nd century by a ditched trackway and traces of habitation (Atkin 1987, 11–14). Pits and ditches found at Coppice Corner, Kingsholm, can be divided into two phases on the basis of ceramics: an earlier group containing just native wares, and a later group which yielded Claudio-Neronian forms paralleled at the Kingsholm fortress (Timby 1999b, 38). The occurrence of a Kingsholm-type flagon in a Period 4.1 pit at the Link Road is significant. Unless it arrived at the site some considerable time after its manufacture it suggests that occupation had commenced by *c*. AD 65, the generally accepted date for the abandonment of the Kingsholm fortress and the end of the pottery industry that supplied it. The fabric has only rarely been identified on sites away from the immediate environs of the fortress (see Timby above), the fort at Cirencester excepted. The Kingsholm kilns were set up expressly to serve the needs of the army (Timby 1990), and the presence of a flagon at the Link Road could suggest that there was a trading or supply link between the fortress and the farmstead. It is possible, although probably unknowable, that the Link Road site lay within the legionary *territorium*, that is land acquired to supply the legion (Hurst 1999a, 127–30 for the most recent discussion of the *territorium* of the later colonia; Mason 1988 for legionary *territoria*). At any rate the site clearly lay within the hinterland (in the modern sense) of Gloucester, and it is quite likely that its growth and development was intimately linked with the supply needs of the army and subsequent town. Equally clearly the inhabitants of the farmstead utilised long-lived pre-existing architectural traditions (mass-built roundhouses), and perhaps, to judge from the mould and loomweight, craft, technological and agricultural ones as well. Regardless of whether the origin of the site pre or post-dated the arrival of the army, it was clearly built in the indigenous tradition rather than being a Roman imposition on the landscape *a novo*.

Period 4.1 probably lasted until at least the late 1st century AD, as Period 4.2 features contained pottery that does not appear before the start of the 2nd century AD at earliest. Excavated features of Period 4.2 formed fenced and ditched enclosures and paddocks, the focus of domestic settlement presumably lying outside the excavated area. It is possible that the cemetery may have started in this period, although it seems to have continued in use until the mid 2nd century. The cemetery, despite its small size (12 individuals), is noteworthy and important in three key respects. First, because of its association with a farmstead, as rural cemeteries are uncommon in Roman Britain. Second, the 2nd-century date for the burial rite adopted (inhumation, in some cases accompanied by grave goods) and third, its composition of adults over the age of 15 who were predominately female. It is worth examining each of these attributes in turn.

The burials can confidently be termed a cemetery as they occupy a discrete area, and show evidence for organisation. The lack of intercutting between graves, and their essentially linear arrangement suggests that the graves were marked and respected. Burials 6 and 14 were laid out side by side, and the skeletal evidence would be consistent with a mature couple. Romano-British rural cemeteries are comparatively rare, if a distinction is drawn between organised nucleated burials and individual or small groups of burials scattered across settlement sites, often within or close to features such as ditches or corn dryers. These latter types of burials are being found in increasing numbers as larger areas of rural sites are excavated. John Pearce (1999) has recently discussed the Hampshire evidence and the interpretation that should be placed upon such burials more generally. It does not necessarily follow that less care was devoted to these burials than to those found in more organised cemeteries. The rarity of rural cemeteries is especially marked in the early Roman period, the principal site to date being Oswlebury, Hampshire, where some 20 Late Iron Age and Early Romano-British cremations were found within an enclosure attached to a farmstead (Collis 1977). Oswlebury stands out as unusual, however, even within a Hampshire context where scattered burials were the norm (Pearce 1999, 153). More directly relevant to the Link Road cemetery is Frocester Court where 60 burials have been found, of which 37 were young infants and 23 children or adults (Price 2000). Frocester is a rare example of a Romano-British villa cemetery, although evidence for rural cemeteries, while by no means ever common, does increase in the late Roman period (Philpott and Reece 1993: Booth's (2001) survey of the Oxfordshire evidence shows no cemeteries at all that can currently be dated to before the 4th century). There were two or three possible Late Iron Age or Early Roman crouched inhumations at Frocester and three mid 3rd-century cremations, the remaining inhumations dating to the late Roman period. Reece (2000) suggests that the burial of infants at Frocester was a constant custom, with adults being disposed of in a way that left no trace until the mid 3rd century when the burial custom changed and adults enter the archaeological record. The lack of early Roman inhumations at Frocester to parallel those at the Link Road is noticeable. The Link Road cemetery is thus clearly unusual, and explanations are necessarily speculative. Could burial within the cemetery, some accompanied by grave goods, have been to affirm a connection with resources and property? Philpott and Reece (1993, 422) have suggested that landowners might maintain a cemetery as a statement of their right to a property, while tenant workers and slaves would not have been buried on land to which they had no lasting attachment.

The second aspect of the cemetery worthy of discussion is the practice of burial by inhumation in the 2nd century, a period when the predominant funerary rite over much of Roman Britain (where evidence survives) was cremation. In the Late Iron Age there was a localised tradition of burial by inhumation, often crouched, in the Cotswold area, the Birdlip burial being the richest and best known example, although there are other examples in the Severn Valley at Barnwood and Beckford (Worcestershire) (Clifford 1930, 224; Whimster 1981, 234). That the tradition of crouched burial continued into the post-Conquest period in the Gloucester region is demonstrated by examples from Wotton, Barnwood and Kingsholm. At the latter site, seven crouched inhumations were found amongst an assemblage of 125 burials dating from the early 2nd to 4th century (Heighway 1980, 57; Garrod and Heighway 1984, 68). Heighway considered that crouched inhumations represent a survival of native tradition, whilst extended burial is more typical of later Roman practice. Of the burials contained in the Link Road cemetery, nos 4, 6, 7, 9, 11, 12, 14 and 15 are essentially crouched, while 3, 13 and 16 are more extended, demonstrating that the native tradition persisted until at least the mid 2nd century AD.

The deposition of grave goods can also be paralleled locally. A burial at Abbeydale Saintbridge contained hob-nailed shoes and a leg and shoulder of lamb, a close parallel for Burial 12 (Garrod and Heighway 1984, 25–6). At Frocester Court a decapitated male contained within a wooden coffin had a leg of lamb placed by the right elbow. The burial (no. 14) is not closely dated within the Roman period (Price 2000, vol. 2, 207). The brooch from Burial 16 is matched by a 1st-century burial at Kingscote, where the brooch also seemingly lay at the feet (Clifford 1963), while the bracelet with Burial 9 can be compared with a burial from 177 Barnwood Road that had an iron bangle on the right wrist. An associated coin of Domitian points to a comparatively early date for this inhumation (Heighway 1980, 62, no. 15). The wooden box that accompanied Burial 15 is harder to match, the tradition of cremation burial accompanied by a wooden box or casket in the early Roman period occurring predominately in the south-east of England (Philpott 1991, 12–21). A late 1st-century cremation in the Wotton cemetery at Gloucester, however, was buried with a wooden box and broken pottery lamps (Heighway 1980, 64). Two burials (3 and 16; two out of the three extended burials in the cemetery) were buried with hob-nailed footware, a tradition which is most commonly found in the 4th century, although odd examples occur with earlier (2nd-century) burials (Philpott 1991, 167). Five burials were contained within wooden coffins to judge from the presence of iron nails at the bottom of the grave fills. Disarticulated animal bones were found scattered within the grave fills, but it is more likely that they were residual material incidentally contained within the grave fill rather than being the remains of a funeral feast.

The third noteworthy facet of the cemetery is its demographic composition (nine females, two males, two unsexed, no children). This suggests that it was not a family group, but rather that the burial population was selected. One of the males (Burial 3) had a very rare deformity to his forearms, a condition that would have been obvious to his contemporaries. In Late Roman inhumation cemeteries males are normally much better represented than females, a phenomenon that is seemingly peculiarly British (see Booth 2001, 29–32 for a summary of recent research). Explanations for this vary, but the unusualness of the Link Road cemetery again needs to be emphasised. It is conceivable that there are further cemeteries, or scattered burials, within the unexcavated parts of the settlement containing the missing males (and infants as at Frocester?), but equally they could have been disposed of in the archaeologically invisible way that was the norm before the advent in the 3rd century of widespread inhumation.

During the earlier 2nd century the farmstead was reorganised (Period 4.3). A 320m-long trackway led to Ermin Street, presumably to separate the passage of stock from arable fields and pastures. At the end of the trackway geophysics suggests a series of paddocks and fields to the east, while to the west Enclosures B–E were examined in the excavation (Fig. 2). Geophysics shows further ditched enclosures to the west of the excavated area, including a curving trackway. Clearly these features cannot be precisely dated, and the evaluation trenches to the west of the excavation area yielded pottery spanning from the 1st to the late 3rd or 4th century (CAT 2000). One possibility is that the curving trackway was replaced by the linear one following the establishment of Ermin Street. Within the excavated area the enclosures presumably performed a variety of agricultural functions, structural evidence being restricted to Structure 6, although even in this case no plan could be reconstructed. The main focus of domestic activity probably lay to the west of the excavated area, and the stone-lined gullies on the very edge of the excavation might point to a possible location for this. A small quantity of roofing tile was recovered from the site, mostly from Period 4.3 contexts, including a couple of fragments of box tile. While the latter must derive from a hypocausted structure, it may not lie in the immediate vicinity as no anomalies were detected in the geophysical survey indicative of a stone villa-type house in the main settlement area. There were no discernible concentrations of tile on the site, most deriving from the infilling of the ditches of Enclosures B and E and ditch 2365.

The Period 4.3 reorganisation had probably taken place by the mid 2nd century AD and Enclosure B was probably replaced by Enclosures D and E during the 3rd century. These enclosures, and Enclosure C, continued in use until at least the late 3rd or early 4th century. Later activity in the general area is suggested by the unstratified coins of AD 313–14 and AD 330–40, and a coin of AD 367–75 from a recut of the trackway ditch shows that this feature remained a visible landscape feature, at least in part, into the late 4th century. The lack of distinctly later 4th-century pottery from the site, however, suggests that domestic activity had ceased by this time. Little can be said about the plan of the farmstead, although the practice of linking a settlement set back from Ermin Street to the road by a ditched trackway is well attested, as at Duntisbourne Leer, Field's Farm and Court Farm Latton (Mudd *et al.* 1999, vol.1, 111, 115–16). At the latter two sites, the trackway seems to date from the 1st century AD.

Work over the last few decades now shows that there was a dense pattern of Romano-British rural settlement in the hinterland of Gloucester east of the Severn (Rawes 1977, 32–9; Rawes 1984, 25; Hurst 1999a, 130, provide references to the sites marked on Fig. 1. For the site discovered in 2001 near Pineholt village hall see Jones 2002). A few high-status villas are known beyond the immediate suburbs of the walled town, at Sandhurst Lane, Wells Bridge and Eastern Radial Road. Further out villas occur at sites such as Hucclecote; possibly Hucclecote bath-house; probably near Upton Lane; Great Witcombe, and Quedgeley Olympus Park, alongside lower-status farmsteads such as Brockworth and the present site. In this context the relationship of the Link Road site with Hucclecote villa, only 650m distant, is worthy of discussion. It is clear from recent work that the masonry villa house at Hucclecote villa was but one part of a complex agricultural landscape. Work in the immediate environs has shown that the house lay within a series of fields and trackways (Sermon 1997) and these clearly extended for some distance. Excavations in 1993 found another stone structure 80m north-east of the villa house, a system of enclosures 150m to the east, and elsewhere a corn dryer and other features (Parry 1994; Parry and Cook 1995). Mrs Clifford (1933) originally proposed that a timber structure was replaced by the masonry villa house around the middle of the 2nd century. There was undoubtedly occupation at the site at this date, as the tile stamped RPG shows, and perhaps earlier to judge from the presence of Flavian samian, but the main floruit of the house occurred in the 4th century, and it may not have been built before the 3rd century at earliest (Branigan 1977, 34; McWhirr 1981, 99). It is conceivable that Hucclecote originated as a similar type of farmstead to Brockworth and the Link Road, but unlike them developed into a villa in the later Roman period (as at Frocester where the villa house replaced a farmstead *c.* AD 275; Price 2000, vol. 1, 87–95). Indeed the development of a villa complex at Hucclecote may account for the limited evidence for 4th-century activity at the present site, the focus of domestic activity shifting to there.

The Romano-British settlement was overlaid by three systems of ridge and furrow which can be related to fields depicted on the Churchdown Tithe Apportionment Map of 1842 (Fig. 3). It is noteworthy that the alignment of the ridge and furrow in the middle field was broadly parallel with the alignment of the Romano-British trackway and enclosures, as medieval fields laid out on a similar alignment to underlying Romano-British sites have been noted elsewhere in the vicinity of Gloucester at Brockworth (Rawes 1981, 45), Upton Lane (Atkin and Garrod 1988, 211), and near Hucclecote villa (Parry 1994, 207). This suggests that the banks and ditches of these Roman field systems survived as sufficiently visible landscape features to influence the orientation of their medieval successors.

BIBLIOGRAPHY

Allason-Jones, L. and Miket, R. 1984 *The catalogue of small finds from South Shields Roman Fort* Soc. Antiq. Newcastle-upon-Tyne Monograph Ser. **2**, Newcastle-upon-Tyne, Society of Antiquaries of Newcastle-upon-Tyne

Allen, J.R.L. and Fulford, M.G. 1996 'The distribution of south-east Dorset Black-Burnished category 1 pottery in south-west Britain', *Britannia* **27**, 223–81

Allen, T.G., Darvill, T.C., Green, L.S. and Jones, M.U. 1993 *Excavations at Roughground Farm, Lechlade, Gloucestershire: a prehistoric and Roman landscape* Thames Valley Landscapes: The Cotswold Water Park **1**, Oxford, Oxford Archaeological Unit

Atkin, M. 1987 'Excavations in Gloucester: an interim report', *Glevensis* **21**, 7–17

Atkin, M. and Garrod, A.P. 1988 'Archaeology in Gloucester 1987: a review', *Trans. Bristol Gloucestershire Archaeol. Soc.* **106**, 209–18

Bagnall Smith, J. 1999 'Votive objects and objects of votive significance from Great Walsingham, Norfolk', *Britannia* **30**, 21–56

Baker, J. and Brothwell, D. 1980 *Animal Diseases in Archaeology* London, Academic Press

Baker, P., Forcey, C., Jundi S. and Witcher R. (eds) 1999 *TRAC 98: Proceedings of the eighth annual theoretical Roman archaeology conference, Leicester 1998* Oxford, Oxbow Books

Barber, A.J. and Walker, G.T. 1998 'Home Farm, Bishop's Cleeve: excavation of a Romano-British occupation site 1993-4', *Trans. Bristol Gloucestershire Archaeol. Soc.* **116**, 117–40

Barclay, A. and Glass, H. 1995 'Excavations of Neolithic and Bronze-Age ring-ditches, Shorncote Quarry, Somerford Keynes, Gloucestershire', *Trans. Bristol and Gloucestershire Archaeol. Soc.* **113**, 21–60

Barclay, A. 1999 'The fired clay', in A. Mudd *et al.* 1999, vol. 2, 421–4

Barford, P. and Hughes, M. 1985 'Other objects of copper alloy', in K. Blockley 1985, 151–72

Barnes, I. (no date) 'The analysis and recreation of bronzes and brass mould residues', in T. Bryce and J. Tate (eds) *The Laboratories of the National Museum of Antiquities of Scotland* **2**, 40–6

Barrett, J.C., Bradley, R. and Green, M. 1991 *Landscape, monuments and society: the prehistory of Cranborne Chase* Cambridge, Cambridge University Press

Bateman, C. 1998 *Gloucester Business Park Link Road, Brockworth, Gloucestershire: archaeological evaluation* unpublished Cotswold Archaeological Trust report no. **98920**

Bateman, C. 1999 *Gloucester Business Park Link Road, Gloucestershire: post-excavation assessment* unpublished Cotswold Archaeological Trust report no. **99980**

Bayley, J. 1992 *Non-ferrous metalworking from Coppergate* The Archaeology of York: The Small Finds **17/7**, London, Council for British Archaeology

Berlin, V., Cusin, V., Viot, G., Girlich, D., Toutain, A., Moncla, A., Vekemans, M., Le Merrer, M., Munnich, A. and Cormier-Daire, V. 1998 'SHOX meutations in dyschondrosteosis (Leri-Weill syndrome)', *Nature Genetics* **19**, 67–9

Besly, E. and Bland, R. 1983 *The Cunetio treasure: Roman coinage of the third century AD* London, British Museum

Blockley, K. 1985 *Marshfield: Ironmongers Piece excavations 1982-3* BAR British Series **141**, Oxford, British Archaeological Reports

Booth, P. 2001 'Late Roman cemeteries in Oxfordshire: a review', *Oxoniensia* **66**, 13–42

Borrill, H. 1981 'The casket burials', in C. Partridge 1981, 304–9

Boyle, A., Jennings, D., Miles, D. and Palmer, S. 1998 *The Anglo-Saxon cemetery at Butler's Field, Lechlade, Gloucestershire. Vol. 1: prehistoric and Roman activity and grave catalogue* Thames Valley Landscapes **10**, Oxford, Oxford Archaeological Unit

Bradley, R. 1981 'Various styles of urns: cemeteries and settlement in southern England c. 1400-1000 BC', in R. Chapman *et al.* (eds) 1981, 93–104

Branigan, K. 1977 *The Roman villa in south-west England* Bradford-on-Avon, Moonraker Press

Brodribb, G. 1989 *Roman brick and tile* Wolfeboro (New Hampshire), Alan Sutton

Brothwell, D. and Higgs, E.S. (eds) 1969 *Science in Archaeology* London, Thames and Hudson

Brown, A.G. and Barber, K.E. 1985 'Late Holocene paleoecology and sediment history of a small lowland catchment in central England', *Quaternary Research* **24**, 87–102

Bruun, P. 1966 *Roman imperial coinage vol. VII: Constantine and Licinius, AD 313–37* London, Spink and Son

Carson, R.A.G., Hill, P.V. and Kent, J.P.C. 1960 *Late Roman bronze coinage, AD 324–491* London, Spink and Son

CAT (Cotswold Archaeological Trust) 2000 *Brockworth MSA, Gloucestershire: archaeological evaluation* unpublished Cotswold Archaeological Trust report no. **001214**

Chapman, R., Kinnes, I. and Ransborg, K. (eds) 1981 *The archaeology of death* Cambridge, Cambridge University Press

Clarke, G. 1979 *Pre-Roman and Roman Winchester, part 2: the Roman cemetery at Lankhills* Winchester Studies **3**, Oxford, Clarendon Press

Clifford, E.M. 1930 'A prehistoric and Roman site at Barnwood, near Gloucester', *Trans. Bristol Gloucestershire Archaeol. Soc.* **52**, 201–54

Clifford, E.M. 1933 'The Roman villa, Hucclecote, near Gloucester', *Trans. Bristol Gloucestershire Archaeol. Soc.* **55**, 323–76

Clifford, E.M. 1954 'The Roman villa, Witcombe, Gloucestershire', *Trans. Bristol Gloucestershire Archaeol. Soc.* **73**, 5–69

Clifford, E.M. 1961 'The Hucclecote Roman villa', *Trans. Bristol Gloucestershire Archaeol. Soc.* **80**, 42–9

Clifford, E.M. 1963 'Burial at Kingscote, Gloucestershire', *Trans. Bristol Gloucestershire Archaeol. Soc.* **82**, 205–7

Collis, J. 1977 'Owslebury (Hants) and the problem of burials on rural settlements', in R. Reece (ed.) 1977, 26–34

Cool, H.E.M. 1990 'Roman metal hair pins from Southern Britain', *Archaeol. J.* **147**, 148–82

Cool, H.E.M. and Mills, J.M. 1993 'The copper alloy and silver grave goods', in D.E. Farwell and T.I. Molleson 1993, 89–96

Cooper, N. 1998 'The supply of pottery to Roman Cirencester', in N. Holbrook (ed.) 1998, 324–50

Crew, P. 1996 *Bloom refining and smithing, slags and other residues* Hist. Metall. Soc. Archaeol. Datasheet **6**, London, Historical Metallurgy Society

Crummy, N. 1983 *The Roman small finds from Excavations in Colchester, 1971-9* Colchester Archaeol. Rep. **2**, Colchester, Colchester Archaeological Trust

Cunliffe, B. 1971 *Excavations at Fishbourne 1961-1969, vol. II: the finds* Rep. Research Committee Soc. Antiq. London **XXVII**, London, Society of Antiquaries

Darling, M.J. 1985 'Roman pottery', in H.R. Hurst 1985, 55–93

Darvill, T.C, Hingley R., Jones, M. and Timby, J. 1986 'A Neolithic and Iron Age site at The Loders, Lechlade, Gloucestershire', *Trans. Bristol Gloucestershire Archaeol. Soc.* **104**, 27–48

Darvill, T. 1987 *Prehistoric Gloucestershire* Gloucester, Alan Sutton/Gloucestershire County Library

Darvill, T. 2000 'Early prehistoric settlement', in E. Price 2000, vol. 1, 193–220

Dixon, P.W. 1973 'Longhouse and roundhouse at Crickley Hill', *Antiquity* **47**, 56–9

Dixon, P. 1994 *Crickley Hill vol. 1: The hillfort defences* Department of Archaeology, University of Nottingham

Driesch, A. von den 1976 *A guide to the measurement of animal bones from archaeological sites* Peabody Museum Bulletin **1**, Harvard, Harvard University

Driesch, A. von den and Boessneck, J. 1974 'Kritische Anmerkungen zur Widerristhohenberechnung aus Langenmassen vor-und Fruhgeschichtlicher', *Saugetierkundiche Mitteilungen* **22** (4), 325–48

Dunning, G.C. 1933 'Report on pottery found in the Crypt Grammar School grounds, Gloucester, during excavations made 1931-2', *Trans. Bristol Gloucestershire Archaeol. Soc.* **55**, 227–91

Dyson, T. (ed.) 1986 *The Roman quay at St Magnus House, London: excavations at New Fresh Wharf, Lower Thames Street, London 1974-8* London Middlesex Archaeol. Soc. Spec. Pap. **8**, London, Museum of London/London and Middlesex Archaeological Society

Ellison, A. 1984 'Bronze Age Gloucestershire: artefacts and distributions', in A. Saville (ed.) 1984a, 113–27

Elsdon, S. 1994 'The Iron Age pottery', in P. Dixon 1994, 203–41

Farwell, D.E. and Molleson, T.I. 1993 *Excavations at Poundbury 1966-80, vol. 2: the cemeteries* Dorset Natur. Hist. Archaeol. Soc. Monograph **11**, Dorchester, Dorset Natural History and Archaeology Society

Fedière, A. (ed.) 1993 *Monde des morts, monde des vivants en Gaule rurale* Tours, FERACF

Fell, C.I. 1961 'Shenberrow Hill Camp, Stanton, Gloucestershire', *Trans. Bristol Gloucestershire Archaeol. Soc.* **80**, 16–41

Foster, J. 1995 'Metalworking in the British Iron Age: the evidence from Weelsby Avenue, Grimsby', in B. Raftery (ed.) 1995, 49–60

Frayer, D.W., Horton, W.A., Macchiarelli, R. and Mussi, M. 1987 'Dwarfism in an adolescent from the Italian late Upper Palaeolithic', *Nature* **330**, 60–3

Garrod, P. and Heighway, C. 1984 *Garrod's Gloucester: archaeological observations 1974-81* Gloucester, Western Archaeological Trust

Grant, A. 1982 'The use of tooth wear as a guide to the age of domestic ungulates', in B. Wilson et al. 1982, 91–108

Gregory, T. 1991 *Excavations in Thetford, 1980-1982, Fison Way* E Anglian Archaeol. Rep. **53**, Dereham, Norfolk Archaeological Unit

Green, G.W. 1992 *Bristol and Gloucester Region (3rd edition)* London, British Geological Survey

GSB (GSB Prospection) 1998 *Brockworth, Gloucestershire* unpublished GSB Prospection report no. 98/35

Harcourt, R.A. 1974 'The dog in prehistoric and early historic Britain', *J. Archaeol. Sci.* **1**, 151–75

Harden, D.B. and Price, J. 1971 'The glass', in B. Cunliffe 1971, 317–58

Hattatt, R. 1987 *Brooches of antiquity* Oxford, Oxbow Books

Hearne, C. and Heaton, M. 1994 'Excavations at a Late Bronze Age settlement in the Upper Thames Valley at Shorncote Quarry near Cirencester, 1992', *Trans. Bristol Gloucestershire Archaeol. Soc.* **112**, 17–57

Hearne, C. and Adam, N. 1999 'Excavation of an extensive Late Bronze-Age settlement at Shorncote Quarry, near Cirencester, 1995-6', *Trans. Bristol Gloucestershire Archaeol. Soc.* **117**, 35–73

Heighway, C.M. 1980 'Roman cemeteries in Gloucester district', *Trans. Bristol Gloucestershire Archaeol. Soc.* **98**, 57–72

Hingley R. 1986 'The Iron Age', in T.C. Darvill *et al.* 1986, 36–43

Holbrook, N. (ed.) 1998 *Cirencester: the Roman town defences, public buildings and shops* Cirencester Excavations **V**, Cirencester, Cotswold Archaeological Trust

Hull, M.R. (forthcoming) *Brooches from pre-Roman and Roman Britain* (typescript in Colchester Museum)

Hunter, A.G. 1963 'Excavations at the Bon Marche site, Gloucester, 1958–59', *Trans. Bristol Gloucestershire Archaeol. Soc.* **82**, 25–65

Hurst, J.D. and Wills, J. 1987 'A 'horn cap' mould from Beckford, Worcestershire', *Proc. Prehist. Soc.* **53**, 492–3

Hurst, H.R. 1985 *Kingsholm* Gloucester Archaeol. Rep. **1**, Gloucester, Gloucester Archaeological Publications

Hurst, H.R. 1999a 'Topography and identity in *Glevum colonia*', in H.R. Hurst (ed.) 1999b, 113–35

Hurst, H.R. (ed.) 1999b *The coloniae of Roman Britain: new studies and a review*, J. Roman Archaeol. Suppl. Ser. **36**, Portsmouth (Rhode Island), Journal of Roman Archaeology

Johns, C. 1996 *The jewellery of Roman Britain* London, UCL Press

Jones, D.M. 1980 *Excavations at Billingsgate Buildings, Lower Thames Street, London, 1974* London Middlesex Archaeol. Soc. Spec. Pap. 4, London, Museum of London/London and Middlesex Archaeological Society

Jones, L. 2002 'Brockworth', in J. Wills (ed.) Archaeological Review 26, *Trans. Bristol Gloucestershire Archaeol. Soc.* **120**, 243

Langer, L.O. 1965 'Dyschondrosteosis, a hereditable bone dysplasia with characteristic roentgenographic features', *American J. Roentgenology* **95**, 178–88

Leach, P. 1982 *Ilchester Vol. 1: Excavations 1974-1975* Western Archaeol. Trust Excav. Monograph Ser. **3**, Gloucester, Alan Sutton

Leach, P. 1998 *Great Witcombe Roman Villa, Gloucestershire: a report on excavations by Ernest Greenfield 1960-1973* BAR British Series **266**, Oxford, British Archaeological Reports

Leah, M. and Young, C.J. 2001 'A Bronze Age burnt mound at Sandy Lane, Charlton Kings, Gloucestershire. Excavations in 1971', *Trans. Bristol Gloucestershire Archaeol. Soc.* **119**, 59–82

MacConnoran, P. 1986 'Footwear', in T. Dyson (ed.) 1986, 218–26

McWhirr, A.D. 1981 *Roman Gloucestershire* Gloucester, Alan Sutton

Manning, W.H. 1985 *Catalogue of the Romano-British iron tools, fittings and weapons in the British Museum* London, British Museum

Mason, D.J.P. 1988 '*Prata legionis* in Britain', *Britannia* **19**, 163–89

Mills, J.M. 1993 'Iron coffin nails and fittings', in D.E. Farwell and T.I. Molleson 1993, 114–27

Morris, E.L. 1994 'Pottery', in C.M. Hearne and M.J. Heaton 1994, 34–43

Mudd A., Williams, R.J. and Lupton, A. 1999 *Excavations alongside Roman Ermin Street, Gloucestershire and Wiltshire: the archaeology of the A419/417 Swindon to Gloucester Road Scheme. Vol 1: Prehistoric and Roman activity; Vol 2: Medieval and post-medieval activity, finds and environmental evidence* Oxford, Oxford Archaeological Unit

O'Connor, T.P. 1990 'Report on the animal bones: the Beeches Nursery field', in R. Reece (ed.) 1990, 20–1

O'Neil, H.E. 1967 'Bevan's Quarry round barrow, Temple Guiting, 1964', *Trans. Bristol Gloucestershire Archaeol. Soc.* **86**, 14–41

Parry, C. 1994 'Hucclecote', in B. Rawes (ed.) Archaeological Review 18, *Trans. Bristol Gloucestershire Archaeol. Soc.* **112**, 206–7

Parry, C. 1998 'Excavations near Birdlip, Cowley, Gloucestershire, 1987-8', *Trans. Bristol Gloucestershire Archaeol. Soc.* **116**, 25–92

Parry, C. and Cook, S. 1995 'Brockworth, Badgeworth, Hucclecote', in B. Rawes (ed.) Archaeological Review 19, *Trans. Bristol Gloucestershire Archaeol. Soc.* **113**, 190

Partridge, C. 1981 *Skeleton Green: a Late Iron Age and Romano-British site* Britannia Monograph Ser. **2**, London, Society for the Promotion of Roman Studies

PCRG (Prehistoric Ceramics Research Group) 1992 *The study of later prehistoric pottery: guidelines for analysis and publication* Prehist. Ceram. Res. Group Occas. Pap. **2**, Oxford, Prehistoric Ceramics Research Group

Peacock, D.P.S. 1967 'Romano-British pottery production in the Malvern district of Worcestershire', *Trans. Worcestershire Archaeol. Soc.* **1**, 15–29

Pearce, J. 1999 'The dispersed dead: preliminary observations on burial and settlement space in rural Roman Britain', in P. Baker *et al.* 1999, 151–62

Philpott, R. 1991 *Burial practices in Roman Britain: a survey of grave treatment and furnishing AD 43–410* BAR British Series **219**, Oxford, British Archaeological Reports

Philpott, R. and Reece, R. 1993 'Sépultures rurales en Bretagne romaine', in A. Fedière (ed.) 1993, 417–23

Price, E. 2000 *Frocester: a Romano-British settlement, its antecedents and successors. Vol. 1: the sites; Vol. 2: the finds* Stonehouse, Gloucester and District Archaeological Research Group

Price, J. and Cottam, S. 1998 'Vessel glass', in P. Leach 1998, 73–81

Purnell, F. and Webb, E.W. 1950 'An Iron Age site near Cheltenham', *Trans. Bristol Gloucestershire Archaeol. Soc.* **69**, 197–9

Raftery, B. (ed.) 1995 *Sites and sights of the Iron Age* Oxbow Monograph **56**, Oxford, Oxbow Books

Rawes, B. 1977 'A Roman site at Wells' Bridge, Barnwood', *Trans. Bristol Gloucestershire Archaeol. Soc.* **95**, 24–39

Rawes, B. 1981 'The Romano-British site at Brockworth, Gloucestershire', *Britannia* **12**, 45–77

Rawes, B. 1984 'The Romano-British site on the Portway, near Gloucester', *Trans. Bristol Gloucestershire Archaeol. Soc.* **100**, 23–72

Rawes, B. 1991 'A prehistoric and Romano-British settlement at Vineyards Farm, Charlton Kings', *Trans. Bristol Gloucestershire Archaeol. Soc.* **109**, 25–89

Reece, R. (ed.) 1977 *Burial in the Roman world* CBA Research Report **22**, London, Council for British Archaeology

Reece, R. (ed.) 1990 *Cotswold Studies II: excavations, survey and records around Cirencester* Cirencester, Cotswold Studies

Reece, R. 2000 'The Frocester cemetery and rural burial in Roman Britain', in Price 2000, vol. 2, 205

Rhodes, M. 1980 'Leather footwear', in D.M. Jones 1980, 99–128

Roe, F. 1998 'Worked stone', in A.J. Barber and G.T. Walker 1998, 128–31

Roe, F. 1999 'The worked stone', in A. Mudd *et al.* 1999, vol. 2, 414–21

Saville, A. (ed.) 1984a *Archaeology in Gloucestershire* Cheltenham, Cheltenham Art Gallery and Museums/Bristol and Gloucestershire Archaeological Society
Saville, A. 1984b 'The Iron Age in Gloucestershire: a review of the evidence', in A. Saville (ed.) 1984a, 140-78
Sermon, R. 1997 'Gloucester Archaeology Unit annual report', *Glevensis* **30**, 41-50
Shers, D.J., Vassal, H.J., Goodman, F.R., Palmer, R.W., Reardon, W., Superti-Furga, A., Scrambler, P.J. and Winter, R.M. 1998 'Mutation and deletion of the pseudoautosomal gene SHOX cause Leri-Weill dyschondrosteosis', *Nature Genetics* **19**, 70-3
Spencer, B. 1983 'Limestone-tempered pottery from South Wales in the Late Iron Age and Early Roman periods', *Bull. Board Celtic Stud.* **30**, 405-19
Spratling, M.G. 1979 'The debris of metalworking', in G.W. Wainwright 1979, 125-49
Stewart, T.D. (ed.) 1970 *Personal identification in mass disasters* Washington, Smithsonian Institution
Taylor, B. and Bagnall, A. 1989 'Finds', in D. Wilson 1989, 35-46
Taylor, B. and Bagnall, A. 1993 'Finds', in D. Wilson 1993, 13-36
Timby, J.R. 1990 'Severn Valley wares: a reassessment', *Britannia* **21**, 243-52
Timby, J.R. 1991 'The Berkeley Street pottery kiln, Gloucester', *J. Roman Pottery Stud.* **4**, 19-31
Timby, J.R. 1998a 'Late Bronze Age/Early Iron Age pottery', in A. Boyle *et al.* 1998, 276-8
Timby, J.R. 1998b *Excavations at Kingscote and Wycomb, Gloucestershire* Cirencester, Cotswold Archaeological Trust
Timby, J.R. 1999a 'Roman pottery from Birdlip Quarry, Cowley', in A. Mudd *et al.* 1999, vol. 2, 339-59
Timby, J.R. 1999b 'Pottery supply to Gloucester colonia', in H.R. Hurst 1999b, 37-44
Timby, J.R. 2001 'The pottery and fired clay', in M. Leah and C.J. Young 2001, 10-17
Timby, J.R. (in prep.) *The pottery from Huntsman Quarry, Naunton, Gloucestershire*
Tomber, R. and Dore, J. 1998 *The national Roman fabric reference collection: a handbook* London, Museum of London Archaeology Service/English Heritage/British Museum
Toynbee, J.M.C. 1973 *Animals in Roman Life and Art* London, Thames and Hudson
Trotter, M. 1970 'Estimation of height from intact limb bones', in T.D. Stewart (ed.) 1970, 71-97
Tylecote, R.F. 1986 *The prehistory of metallurgy in the British Isles* London, Institute of Metals
Wainwright, G.W. 1979 *Gussage All Saints: an Iron Age settlement in Dorset* Dept Environ. Archaeol. Rep. **10**, London, HMSO
Walker, G. Thomas, A. and Bateman, C. (forthcoming) 'Bronze-Age and Romano-British sites excavated on the route of the Tewkesbury Eastern Relief Road, Gloucestershire, 1996-7', *Trans. Bristol Gloucestershire Archaeol. Soc.*
Whimster, R. 1981 *Burial Practices in Iron Age Britain* BAR British Series **90**, Oxford, British Archaeological Reports
Williams, J.H. 1971 'Roman building materials in the South-West', *Trans. Bristol Gloucestershire Archaeol. Soc.* **90**, 95-119
Wilson, B., Grigson, C. and Payne, S. (eds) 1982 *Ageing and sexing animal bones from archaeological sites* BAR British Series **109**, Oxford, British Archaeological Reports
Wilson, D. 1989 *Excavation of a Romano-British villa at Wortley, Gloucestershire* Fifth Interim Report, Department of Adult and Continuing Education, University of Keele
Wilson, D. 1993 *Excavation of a Romano-British villa at Wortley, Gloucestershire* Ninth Interim Report, Department of Adult and Continuing Education, University of Keele

Wilthew, P., Bayley, J. and Linton, R. 1991 'Analysis of the metal-working debris', in T. Gregory 1991, 141–3

Woodward, A. 1998 'Bronze Age pottery', in C. Parry 1998, 66–7

WEA (Workshop of European Anthropologists) 1980 'Recommendation for age and sex diagnosis of skeletons', *J. Hum. Evol.* **9**, 517–49

Young, C.J. 1977 *Oxfordshire Roman pottery* BAR British Series **43**, Oxford, British Archaeological Reports